Accelerate

A SKILLS-BASED
SHORT COURSE

UPPER-INTERMEDIATE

Series editor: Philip Prowse

JACKY NEWBROOK • NIGEL NEWBROOK • WITH NICK KENNY

Heinemann English Language Teaching, Oxford

A division of Macmillan Publishers Limited

Companies and representatives throughout the world

ISBN 0 435 28269 7

Text © Nigel Newbrook and Jacky Newbrook
with Nick Kenny 1995
Design and illustration © Macmillan Publishers Limited
1998

Heinemann is a registered trademark of Reed Educational & Professional Publishing Limited

First published 1995

All rights reserved; no part of this publication may be reproduced, stored in a retrieval system, or transmitted in any form or by any means, electronic, mechanical, photocopying, recording or otherwise, without the prior written permission of the publishers.

Designed by Ken Vail Graphic Design
Cover design by Threefold Design
Cover photograph by Frank Orel/Tony Stone Images
Illustrated by: Archer Art (Len Jan Vis)' Jo Dennis; Garden Studio (Robert Stockdale); Simon Girling & Assoc. (Mike Lacey); Ed McLachlan; Gillian Martin; Toney Randell; Linda Rogers Assoc. (Tony Morris); Martin Sanders; Lisa Smith' Specs Art (Richard Berridge).

Photographs by Fortean Picture Library p12; The Ronald Grant Archive p8, 26; The Image Bank p16; Colin Bowers/Reflections p18, 72; South American Pictures p17; Stockingfillas Catalogue p48; Tony Stone Images p22, 33, 44(r); The Telegraph Colour Library p44(l); Rebekah Trolley p36; Helene Rogers/W R Matthews/Ron Keadman/Tripp p6, 28, 56, 90.

Commissioned photography by Chris Honeywell pp32, 34, 35 48

The authors would like to thank Neil and Ralph Newbrook.

They would also like to thank Jill Barlett, Marc Beeby, David Ieuan Bowen, PC Don Cahill, Gillie Cunningham, Robin Davis, Jennifer Hinch, Francoise Mouchet, Roger Owens, Andrea Reed.

The publishers would like to thank Helena Gomm, Mel Watson and Fiona Clegg.

The authors and publishers would like to thank the following for permission to reproduce their material: Reginald Maddock for the extract from `Dragon in the garden' reproduced by permission of the Estate of Reginald Maddock and John Johnson (Authors' Agent) Ltd; Chatto & Windus for the extract `The Rebel' by D J Enright from `Rhyme Times Rhyme' reproduced by permission of Watson, Little Ltd; HarperCollins Publishers Limited for the extract from `Modern Mysteries of Britain' by Janet and Colin Bord; Michael Joseph Ltd and Penguin Books Ltd for `The Landlady' from `Kiss Kiss' by Roald Dahl; Reed Consumer Books for the extracts from `Myths and Legends' by Ridden & Lewis published by Dean Read Int Books Ltd (C. Hamlyn ©1987); *Chat* for the quiz on page 49; Octopus Books Ltd for `Amazing Flops and Fiascos' by Brenda Apsley and `Amazing Blunders and Bungles' by Peter Eldin; *Daily Mail* for `Psst... have you heard the truth about rumours' by George Gorden 117191, reproduced by permission of Solo Syndications; *The European* for `Memories are really made of this' by Jeremy Lawrence l~16l6l91; Dr Sidney Simon for the extract from `Change your life now'.

While every effort has been made to trace the owners of copyright material in this book, there have been some cases when the publishers have been unable to contact the owners. We should be grateful to hear from anyone who recognises their copyright material and who is unacknowledged. We shall be pleased to make the necessary amendments in future editions of this book.

Printed in Scotland by Cambus Litho

98 99 00 01 02 11 10 9 8 7 6 5 4 3 2

Contents

Map of the book

Unit 1
Out of place
Lesson 1 New beginnings — 6
Lesson 2 Why should I? — 8
Lesson 3 Teenagers! — 10

Unit 2
Mysteries
Lesson 1 Unidentified flying objects — 12
Lesson 2 Ghosts — 14
Lesson 3 Pyramids and lines — 16

Unit 3
A place to stay
Lesson 1 Find your own lodgings — 18
Lesson 2 'I'll give you a nice cup of tea …' — 20
Lesson 3 'The perfect age!' — 22

Unit 4
Legends and heroes
Lesson 1 '…and they lived happily ever after' — 24
Lesson 2 Robbing the rich to give to the poor — 26
Lesson 3 The girl who heard voices — 28

Unit 5
Fire and theft
Lesson 1 The work of a moment — 30
Lesson 2 A puff of smoke — 32
Lesson 3 A crime or a joke? — 34

Unit 6
Have you got a problem?
Lesson 1 Strange obsessions — 36
Lesson 2 To buy or not to buy? — 38
Lesson 3 Nothing but the truth — 40

Unit 7
Deceits, tricks and blunders
Lesson 1 Never trust a stranger — 42
Lesson 2 They all look the same — 44
Lesson 3 Where there's smoke, there's fire — 46

Unit 8
All in the mind
Lesson 1 I think, therefore … — 48
Lesson 2 It's the way you use it — 50
Lesson 3 It's on the tip of my tongue — 52

Unit 9
Confidence
Lesson 1 Recognising yourself — 54
Lesson 2 Thinking positively — 56
Lesson 3 Expressing yourself — 58

Unit 10
The right thing to do
Lesson 1 The morning — 60
Lesson 2 The evening — 62
Lesson 3 The next day — 64

Practice pages — 66

Map of the book

	Language focus	Skills focus
Unit 1 *Out of place*		
Lesson 1 New beginnings Experience of the first day in a new place	Past simple and past continuous	**Reading:** for main ideas and detail **Listening** for main ideas **Speaking:** fluency
Lesson 2 Why should I? Rebels and rebellion	Present simple and present continuous with present meaning	**Speaking:** giving opinions **Listening and writing** to complete a poem
Lesson 3 Teenagers! Conflicts between parents and teenagers	*Will* for predictions *Will* for annoying habits	**Reading** and reacting to a poem **Listening** for main ideas and specific information
Unit 2 *Mysteries*		
Lesson 1 Unidentified flying objects Do UFOs exist?	Present perfect simple Present perfect and past simple The gerund as subject	**Reading:** ordering a text **Listening** for main ideas and detail **Speaking:** conducting an interview
Lesson 2 Ghosts Strange experiences	Direct and indirect questions Negative words used for emphasis	**Listening** for specific information **Writing** a narrative composition
Lesson 3 Pyramids and lines Two of the world's greatest mysteries	Past passive Modal verbs: deductions and speculations in the past	**Reading** to complete a table **Listening** for main ideas and detail **Speaking:** giving explanations
Unit 3 *A place to stay*		
Lesson 1 Find your own lodgings Short story: part 1	Order of adjectives Subclauses without verbs	**Reading and listening** for main ideas and detail; predicting
Lesson 2 'I'll give you a nice cup of tea …' Short story: part 2	Question tags Intensifiers: *so, such, do*	**Speaking:** predicting **Reading and listening** for specific information
Lesson 3 'The perfect age!' Short story: part 3	Short answers: *so am I, neither do I* Adverbials: modifications of degree	**Reading and listening** for specific information; predicting
Unit 4 *Legends and heroes*		
Lesson 1 '… and they lived happily ever after' Legends from around the world	Past simple and past perfect Narrative time markers	**Speaking:** storytelling **Reading and listening** for gist **Writing:** a narrative composition
Lesson 2 Robbing the rich to give to the poor The life of Robin Hood	*Used to* and past simple *Used to* and *would*	**Reading:** ordering a text; completing a text **Listening** for main ideas
Lesson 3 The girl who heard voices The story of Joan of Arc	Impersonal passive	**Listening** for specific information **Speaking:** making a radio programme
Unit 5 *Fire and theft*		
Lesson 1 The work of a moment Witness to a crime	Reported speech: changes to the verb Temporal changes to words	**Listening** for main ideas and detail **Writing:** taking notes
Lesson 2 A puff of smoke A dangerous job	Reported speech: questions Reporting verbs	**Listening** for main ideas: note-taking **Speaking:** roleplaying a conversation
Lesson 3 A crime or a joke? The travels of a garden gnome	Definite, indefinite and zero articles	**Listening and reading** to order and complete a text

	Language focus	Skills focus
Unit 6 *Have you got a problem?*		
Lesson 1 Strange obsessions Collecting unusual items	Relative pronouns Relative clauses	**Reading** for specific information **Listening** to complete a table
Lesson 2 To buy or not to buy? Compulsive shopping	Ways of giving advice	**Reading** a questionnaire; for gist **Listening**: inferring
Lesson 3 Nothing but the truth A moral dilemma	First conditional Second conditional	**Reading** for specific information **Speaking**: roleplaying a court scene
Unit 7 *Deceits, tricks and blunders*		
Lesson 1 Never trust a stranger A short story	Present participles	**Reading** for main ideas; inferring **Listening**: ordering events **Writing**: descriptions
Lesson 2 They all look the same, A newspaper report about a terrible mistake	Third conditional *Should(n't) have*	**Reading**: ordering a text; for specific information **Listening**: taking notes
Lesson 3 Where there's smoke, there's fire How rumours spread	Revision of passive: passive form of verbs Passive form of modal verbs	**Listening** for gist **Reading** for main ideas **Speaking**: talking about urban myths
Unit 8 *All in the mind*		
Lesson 1 I think, therefore … The brain and gender	Comparative forms of adjectives Comparisons: equality and inequality Comparisons: adverbs	**Listening** for main ideas **Reading** and answering a quiz
Lesson 2 It's the way you use it Problem solving and lateral thinking	Conditional sentences in reported speech	**Reading** for main ideas **Listening**: problem solving
Lesson 3 It's on the tip of my tongue Ways to improve your memory	Verbs with infinitive and *-ing* form	**Reading** to complete a text and for main ideas **Speaking**: exchanging information
Unit 9 *Confidence*		
Lesson 1 Recognising yourself How confident are you?	Reflexive verbs Verbs and preposition combinations	**Listening** for main ideas and detail **Reading** and answering a quiz
Lesson 2 Thinking positively How a man overcame fear	Modal verbs: *can/be able to* Modal verbs: *need/don't need/needn't*	**Listening** for specific information **Reading** for main ideas and detail
Lesson 3 Expressing yourself Finding the right words	Adverbs of frequency Adverbs of manner *It's time* + past tense (subjunctive)	**Reading** for main ideas **Writing**: dialogues **Listening**: completing a table
Unit 10 *The right thing to do*		
Lesson 1 The morning Short story: part 1	Time clauses with *before, after, once* Clauses with *having* Past continuous for future in the past	**Reading** for main ideas; predicting **Listening** for gist
Lesson 2 The evening Short story: part 2	Conjuctions: *if* replacements Conjuctions: *although* and *despite/in spite of*	**Reading and listening** for specific information
Lesson 3 The next day Short story: part 3	Present wishes Past regrets	**Reading** for specific information **Speaking**: roleplaying a conversation

Unit 1 Out of place

Lesson 1 *New beginnings*

Language focus: Past simple and past continuous

Skills focus:
Reading for main ideas and detail
Listening for main ideas
Speaking: fluency

1

Work in groups. Look at the following situations. How many have you experienced? Make a list of adjectives to describe how you felt or how you think you would feel in each of the situations.

– your first day in a new job
– your first day in a new school
– going on holiday alone
– going to a party alone
– going to the cinema alone
– your first day in a new country
– being in a strange city

Now look at the words below, and compare them with your list. Which words are positive and which are negative? Which is the strongest positive word and which is the strongest negative word?

> afraid   anxious   apprehensive   confused
> delighted   embarrassed   enthusiastic   excited
> happy   lonely   panic-stricken   pleased
> sad   surprised   vulnerable

2

Read the text, which describes a boy's first day at a new school. Work in pairs and decide which of the words below fit each section of the text best.

> anticipation   confusion   dislike
> isolation   loneliness

A   I'd never seen Cronton School until the morning I started there. My mother took me in the car, dropping me at the gate.

She grinned at me and said, 'Now it's up to you.' I walked straight in, looking forward in an odd, excited way to being the same as other kids. The school was just as my mother had described it, a group of buildings made of concrete and glass, with an overgrown playing-field behind it stretching away into the distance where the hills were.

B   I walked along the front of the school and round a corner and I was in the playground. In front of me were hundreds of children doing the things I had never done. They were wrestling and rolling and screaming and shouting. They were running about so swiftly that they made me feel dizzy, while their noise deafened me.

UNIT 1 LESSON 1

C   In a corner of the playground I felt loneliness for the first time in my life. Loneliness isn't being alone, but wondering why you have to be alone. I had rarely known other kids, I had always been alone, yet in those first moments at school I felt loneliness flood through me as I watched the hundreds of children. They and I were all wearing the same uniform, but they were different from me. They were rough savages, screaming their war-cries and rushing into battle, and they were happy in a way I had never known. They were happy shouting at each other, wrestling with each other, hating each other.

D   Then one of them spotted me and, like a dog catching a strange scent, he stopped in front of me. He was smaller than I was and younger, and his thick glasses gave him the look of an owl.
   'You a new kid?' he asked.
I nodded.
   'What's your name?'
   'Stewart,' I said.
   'Stewart what?' he asked.
   'Jimmy Stewart.'
'Jimmy Stewart,' he said as if tasting the name. Then he went into a dance and started screaming, 'Jimmy Stewpot! Jimmy Stewpot!'

E   I was so astonished that I just stared at him and didn't at first see the other boys his voice had attracted. They came gathering round and while he went on dancing and jumping, they studied me. He was red-faced and hoarse, his spectacles were on the end of his nose, he was a nightmare of a boy, yet they watched me.

'He's a new kid!' he yelled. 'His name's Jimmy Stewpot!'

I could see dozens of pairs of eyes and I knew how zoo animals must feel on Sunday afternoons when people press close to the cages. There was a dull kind of interest in all the eyes, interest and animosity, but no friendliness. I felt lonelier than ever.

3

Look at these words from the text and complete the table with the correct noun or adjective forms.

Adjective	Noun
lonely	loneliness
excited	
happy	
astonished	
	interest
	friendliness

4

In pairs discuss these questions about the text.

1 Why is the boy upset when he first enters the playground?
2 How does he describe the children already there?
3 Why does the smaller boy shout at him?
4 Why does he compare himself with animals at the zoo?

5

Listen to Neil, Karen and Lisa talking about their first day at school, and make notes about how they each felt on their first day at school and why, and what happened.

Compare your answers in pairs.

6

Work in pairs. Talk about your first day at school. Compare your experiences with those of Neil, Karen and Lisa. Were their experiences similar to yours?

Homework

Choose one situation from Activity 1. Write a paragraph of about 50 words describing how you felt. Use the list of adjectives that you made in Activity 1 to help you.

Language Summary

Past simple and past continuous
   I **walked** along the front of the school.
   They **were wrestling** and **rolling** and **screaming** and **shouting**.
   It **was raining** when I **walked** to school.

see practice page 66

Unit 1 Out of place

Lesson 2 *Why should I?*

Language focus:	Present simple and continuous with present meaning
Skills focus:	Speaking: giving opinions Listening and writing to complete a poem

1

Look at the photo of James Dean in the film *Rebel Without a Cause*. James Dean plays a teenager who rebels against authority. In groups, decide which of the words in the box you would use to describe a rebel. Do you think it is a good thing or a bad thing to be a rebel?

> cheeky conformist exciting fun mischievous
> naughty noisy obedient polite rude
> tactless troublesome unhappy

2

In groups, decide how far you agree with these statements. Give your reasons. Complete the final sentence with a definition that most people in your group agree with.

1 Rebelling against rules is a natural part of growing up.
2 You should always accept rules laid down by society.
3 Rules are made to be broken.
4 School rules are often silly and need not be obeyed.

A rebel is _____

3

In the same groups, list as many ways as you can of how people show rebellion. Which of your ideas do you think are serious and which are not so serious?

UNIT 1 LESSON 2

4

The poem is about a rebel like James Dean, and describes the ways in which he rebels. In pairs, imagine how the sentences end and complete the poem.

5

 Listen to the poem, and see if your ideas were right.

6

In pairs, decide how much of a rebel the boy in the poem actually is. Discuss why do you think he is doing these things? Think about his background and imagine what his life is like.

What do you think the last two lines of the poem mean? How far does this description of a rebel fit the definition you wrote in Activity 2? *Discuss*

7

Listen to Susan, Robin and Lynne talking about their own rebellious times. Make notes under the following headings:

How old were they when they were rebels?
Why did they rebel?
What did they do?
How did they feel?

Work in pairs and compare your notes. Have you or your partner ever done anything rebellious?

8

Work in groups and discuss which of the three speakers would be considered the most rebellious in your country. Give reasons for your choice. What behaviour is considered to be rebellious in your country?

Homework

Write ten rules for being a successful rebel.

Example: When someone tells you to do something, do the opposite.

The Rebel

When everybody has short hair,
The rebel *lets his hair grow long.*

When everybody has long hair,
The rebel *cuts his hair short.*

When everybody talks during the lesson,
The rebel *doesn't say a word.*

When nobody talks during the lesson,
The rebel *creates a disturbance.*

When everybody wears a uniform,
The rebel *dresses in fantastic clothes.*

When everybody wears fantastic clothes,
The rebel *dresses soberly.*

In the company of dog lovers,
The rebel *expresses a preference for cats.*

In the company of cat lovers,
The rebel *expresses a preference for dogs.*

When everybody is praising the sun,
The rebel *remarks on the need for rain.*

When everybody is greeting the rain,
The rebel *regrets the absence of sun.*

When everybody goes to the meeting,
The rebel *stays at home and reads a book.*

When everybody stays at home and reads a book,
The rebel *goes to the meeting.*

When everybody says, Yes, please,
The rebel *says No thankyou.*

When everybody says, No, thank you,
The rebel *says yes please.*

It's very good that we have rebels,
You may not find it very good to be one.

Language Summary

Present simple and present continuous with present meaning

Everybody **wears** a uniform.
Everybody **is praising** the sun.

see practice page 67

Unit 1 Out of place

Lesson 3 *Teenagers!*

Language focus: *Will* for predictions
Will for annoying habits

Skills focus: Reading and reacting to a poem
Listening for main ideas and specific information

1

Look at these words. In pairs, discuss which ones you would use to talk about a teenager and which you would use to talk about a parent.

> contradict   interfering   nagging   scruffy
> surly   tidy   unreasonable

Youth is a person

Youth is a person
Youth is a clan,
Youth is a child, yet
Youth is a man.

Youth is a group of unruly yobs,
Youth has no respect and above all no jobs.
Youth has no morals, youth has no rules,
Youth only revolts; They should cane them
    at schools.

When youth cries out 'aggro'
And violently fights,
The people 'tut tut', say, 'this is not right'.
But when youth cries out 'peace',
And asks for the same,
The people then say, 'what a cowardly game'.

No wonder youth in society's cell
Cries, 'Please for an end to this unfair hell'.

2

Work in pairs. Read the poem written by a teenager and answer the questions.

1 What opinions are being expressed?
2 Do you think most teenagers feel like this?
3 The poem was written in the 1960s. Have things changed for teenagers since then?

3

Form two groups. Group A make a list of typical complaints that parents make about teenagers.
Group B make a list of typical complaints that teenagers make about parents. Then find a partner from the other group and compare your points.

4

Listen to the first part of this radio programme about teenagers. Number the words from Activity 1 in the order that you hear them.

Are any of the complaints you listed in Activity 3 mentioned? What other points are mentioned?

5

Work in groups. Discuss which is more difficult, being a parent of a teenager or being a teenager.

6

Part two of the programme is an interview with a youth worker. In pairs, decide what you think a youth worker does. Do you have youth workers in your country? Listen and answer these questions.

1 What does a youth worker do?
2 What doesn't a youth worker do?
3 Do you think it's a good idea to have youth workers?

UNIT 1 LESSON 3

7

What do you think are the real causes of conflict between parents and teenagers? Make a list of possible explanations with your partner.

Listen to part three of the programme and compare your list with the reasons mentioned by the youth worker.

8

In part four of the programme the youth worker talks about possible solutions to the problem of conflict between teenagers and their parents. Look at the following solutions and tick the ones you think he will mention. Then listen to part four. Were you right? Which of the solutions do you agree with?

1 Young people should obey their parents or leave home. ☐
2 Parents should be more strict with teenagers and should insist that they obey their rules. ☐
3 Parents should try to involve teenagers more in decision making. ✓
4 Young people should leave home as soon as they can. ☐
5 Parents should not try to impose their ideas on teenagers. ✓
6 Teenagers should be allowed to make rules for their own behaviour. ✓
7 Both parents and young people should try to understand each other's points of view. ✓
8 Both parents and teenagers should talk about their problems. ✓

Homework

Look at this example of a description of an ideal parent:

Patient
Always there
Reliable
Easygoing
Never unfair
Trusting

Now use the letters of the word TEENAGER to describe your idea of an ideal teenager, or, if you prefer, the worst kind of teenager!

Language Summary

Will for predictions
   I think it **will** always happen.

Will for annoying habits *always*
   Why **will** they always contradict everything you say? *keeps on + vb + ing*

see practice page 68

Unit 2 Mysteries

Lesson 1 *Unidentified flying objects*

Language focus: Present perfect simple
Present perfect and past simple
The gerund as subject

Skills focus: Reading: ordering a text
Listening for main ideas and detail
Speaking: conducting an interview

1

The woman who took the photograph on the right believes that it shows an alien spaceship (an unidentified flying object or UFO). How many other explanations can you think of for the image in the photograph?

2

Work in pairs. Read this text about UFOs and put the paragraphs in the correct order. Number them 1 to 5.

A
Or is it possible that UFOs are not from a different dimension, but are simply hallucinations, creations of the human mind? This may be so, but explaining why they are sometimes seen by several people at once is hard; they show up on radar and they sometimes leave tangible evidence behind them. We know that the mind can play strange tricks, but can it impose hallucinations on other people's minds as well?

B
UFOs are usually assumed to come from outer space, from civilisations considerably more advanced technologically than our own. They are crewed by space-beings, who either look like us or are able to adopt a human disguise. They come here, according to various theories, to investigate our planet and its inhabitants, to collect specimens, and to spy out the land for invasion.

C
One suggestion connected to the hallucination theory is that humans have a need to believe in a superior supernatural power, and with the decline of the established religions, people have turned to belief in UFOs, seeing them as vehicles of powerful beings in the sky. It is said that people's need to see UFOs is so strong that it actually causes them to appear in the sky.

D
Unfortunately, none of the people who claims to have been on board a UFO has ever brought back as a souvenir an object not manufactured on earth, nor has any UFO ever left such an object behind it. There is also the problem of the enormous distances involved. The nearest star-system which might have life in it is Alpha Centauri, and even if a spacecraft from that system had a speed of seventy million miles per hour, it would still take it almost a hundred years to fly to the earth and back again.

E
An alternative theory, which gets round the problem of distance, is that UFOs come from a different dimension altogether, not governed by the scientific rules of time and distance that we know. This would explain why they suddenly appear out of nowhere and disappear into nowhere again. According to this theory, UFOs belong to a place beyond our comprehension, and trying to describe them in terms of our scientific laws is meaningless.

UNIT 2 LESSON 1

3

Find the word in the text that means:

Paragraph **A**
1 something that can be touched (noun)
2 false impressions in your mind (noun)

Paragraph **B**
3 a false appearance (noun)
4 believed (verb)

Paragraph **E**
5 a way of measuring time and space (noun)

4

You are going to hear Roger talking about his sighting of a possible UFO. As you listen, look at the pictures of UFOs. Which picture illustrates what Roger saw?

5

Listen to Roger again and decide if the following statements are true or false.

1 Roger was out walking with his family. ☐
2 Roger saw some strange lights from the top of a bus. ☐
3 Roger saw some lights going up the hill and climbing into the sky. ☐
4 Roger was worried when he saw the lights. ☐
5 Roger's parents confirmed what he had seen. ☐
6 Roger and his parents were very excited that evening. ☐
7 The newspaper report made Roger think that it must have been a UFO. ☐

6

Listen to Andrea, who does not believe in UFOs. Make a note of three points she makes against the existence of UFOs. Do you agree with her?

7

In pairs, write questions to ask other students about their belief in UFOs. Use your questions to find out how many students in your class believe in UFOs and how many do not. Make sure you ask them why and note down their reasons.

Homework

Write a paragraph summing up your survey on your class's views on UFOs. Try to connect your sentences with phrases such as:

On the one hand,
On the other hand,
On balance, therefore,
However,
Nevertheless,

Language Summary

Present perfect simple
   People **have turned** to belief in UFOs.
   There **have been** many sightings in recent years.
   I**'ve** never actually **seen** anything like a UFO myself.

Present perfect and past simple
   I **have seen** a UFO.
   When I was 17 I **saw** a UFO.

The gerund as subject
   Explaining why they are sometimes seen by several people at once is hard.

see practice page 69

Unit 2 Mysteries

Lesson 2 *Ghosts*

Language focus: Direct and indirect questions
Negative words used for emphasis
Skills focus: Listening for specific information
Writing: a narrative composition

1

Close your eyes and listen to the music. How does it make you feel? Write down some adjectives to describe your feelings. In pairs, compare the words you have thought of.

2

Work in pairs. Look at the picture, which shows a strange experience. Find these objects in the picture: helmet, shield, sword, feathers.

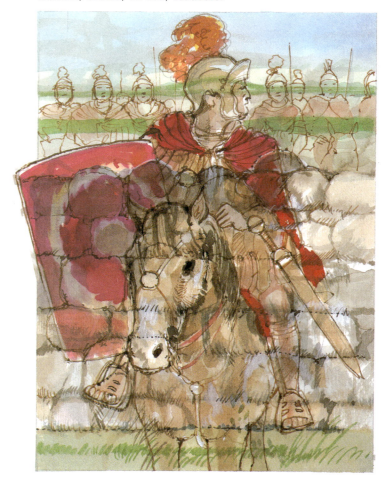

3

You are going to hear Harry Martindale talking about the strange experience in the picture. Before you listen write five questions to ask him about this experience.

Listen to the tape. Were your questions answered?

4

Number the statements below in the order they happened.

a Harry noticed that all the soldiers had helmets on.
b He heard a musical note like a trumpet.
c He collapsed at the top of the cellar steps.
d He couldn't hear any speech, just a murmuring noise.
e He saw a soldier on horseback.
f He fell off his ladder and ran into the corner.

Listen to Harry again and check your answers.

5

Read the text about Harry's experience. There are six mistakes in it. Underline the mistakes and correct them according to what Harry said. Check your answers in pairs.

> When Harry was 18, and learning to be a carpenter, he was installing central heating in the Treasurer's House in Edinburgh. Suddenly, he heard the noise of a musical note, which seemed to be like the beating of a drum. At the same time, he saw the head of a Roman soldier, and was rather surprised. Other soldiers followed – about 50 altogether – and Harry noticed that, although they seemed to be perfectly normal, he could, in fact, see right through them.

6

Do you believe in ghosts? In groups find out if anyone has ever had a ghostly experience or knows anyone who has.

7

In pairs, invent your own ghost story. Make notes using these questions to help you.

Who is involved?
Where does the action take place?
When did it happen?
What exactly happened?
What did the people in the story do?
What happened next?
What was the result?
Does the story have a happy or sad ending?

You might like to use some of the vocabulary below.

> apparition atmosphere bang chains
> to creak darkness to float floorboard
> footstep ghostly headless mysterious
> to rattle to scream shocked silence white

Homework

Write your ghost story from Activity 7 in 180 words. Give it an interesting title.

Language Summary

Direct questions
  How old were you when you saw the ghosts?
  Did you get a good view of them?

Indirect questions
  Did he say how old he was when he saw the ghosts?
  Did you ask him if he got a good view of them?

Negative words used for emphasis
  I was in **no** fit state to count them.
  Not one of them looked in my direction.
  The horses were **nothing** like the ones they use nowadays on TV.

see practice page 70

Unit 2 Mysteries

Lesson 3 Pyramids and lines

Language focus: Past passive
Modal verbs: deductions and speculations in the past

Skills focus: Reading to complete a table
Listening for main ideas and detail
Speaking: giving explanations

1

Work in pairs. Discuss what you know about Tutankhamun. Have you heard of the curse of Tutankhamun? What do you know about it?

2

Read the text and find out whether the author believes in the curse of Tutankhamun. Give reasons for your answer.

Perhaps the best-known 'mystery' of the Land of the Pharaohs is the story of the curse of Tutankhamun's tomb.

In 1922 the tomb of Pharaoh Tutankhamun, who died aged 18 in 1353 BC, was discovered in the Valley of the Kings at Luxor in Egypt, by Lord Carnarvon and Howard Carter.

On a wall in the tomb, a curse was written in hieroglyphics: 'Death will destroy whoever disturbs the pharaoh's peace'. However, this did not frighten Carnarvon or Carter. They opened the innermost part of the tomb in February 1923, in the presence of about 20 people, and found the mummy of Tutankhamun and an astounding quantity of treasure.

Carnarvon, who was 56, died of pneumonia in Cairo within two months. For unexplained reasons, all the lights in Cairo flickered out at about the moment of his death, and then went on again. By 1929, it is claimed, 22 people who had been involved with Tutankhamun's mummy had died prematurely, 13 of whom had witnessed the opening of the tomb. Hollywood producers were inspired to create a series of horror films on the theme of 'the mummy's curse'.

If the curse really worked, as some people like to think, the obvious question is, why did it not strike down the others who were involved, including Howard Carter, the effective leader of the enterprise, who died at the reasonably ripe age of 65 in 1939? Other fanciful theories have been rejected on similar grounds, such as the Egyptian priests concealing poisons or radioactive materials in the tombs, or somehow making use of lethal cosmic rays. A more sensible theory is that bacteria was a possible cause of premature death. A Cairo University biologist, Ezzeddin Taha, who examined the mummy, suggested this in 1962; and soon afterwards died prematurely himself. He was killed in a car crash, but his death led to claims that the priests of ancient Egypt had struck again.

3

Look back at the text and match the words on the left with the correct definition on the right.

1 curse
2 hieroglyphics
3 astounding
4 flickered
5 prematurely
6 ripe
7 fanciful

a before (their) natural time
b unrealistic
c (here) old
d flashed and then died away
e amazing
f a statement intended to bring evil or bad luck to someone else
g ancient Egyptian writing system

4

Work in pairs and complete the table below.

Name	Date of death	Age at death	Link with curse	Logical reason
Carnarvon				
	1962			
		65		

UNIT 2 LESSON 3

5

Discuss whether you believe the logical explanations which are given in the text. Do you think there may be something mysterious about the deaths?

6

The photo below shows another of the world's great mysteries. In pairs, discuss what you think it is.

7

Listen to the description of the Nazca Lines in Peru. In pairs, decide which of the following summaries best matches what you heard. Say what is wrong with the other two summaries.

1 The lines were made by taking stones out of the soil. There are hundreds of figures of birds, fish and cats. They can be seen clearly on the ground.
2 The lines were made by making animal shapes out of stones placed on the soil. The lines need to be viewed from the air in order to see the shapes properly.
3 The lines were made by taking stones out of the ground, thereby revealing the soil below. There are various different animal figures, none of which can be viewed properly at ground level.

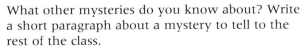

What other mysteries do you know about? Write a short paragraph about a mystery to tell to the rest of the class.

8

Discuss the following in groups: Why would people nearly two thousand years ago make patterns which can only be seen from the air? The illustrations below may give you some ideas to include in your discussion. Decide on the best theory, giving your reasons.

1 Ancient runways for the gods to land.
2 Pathways to sacred temples.
3 Launch pads for balloons taking dead Nazcan chiefs on their last journey to the sun.

Language Summary

Past passive
  The tomb **was discovered** by Lord Carnavon and Howard Carter.
  A curse **was written** in hieroglyphics.
  The lines **were made** by taking stones out of the soil.

Modal verbs: deductions and speculations in the past
  They **must have taken** a long time to make.
  They **could have been** runways for gods to land.
  They **may have been** launch pads for balloons.
  They **might have been** pathways to temples.
  They **can't have served** any practical purpose.

see practice page 71

Unit 3 A place to stay

Lesson 1 *Find your own lodgings*

Language focus: Order of adjectives
Subclauses without verbs
Skills focus: Reading and listening for main ideas and detail; predicting

1

The city of Bath is in south-west England. Have you ever been there? What do you know about the city? Look at the information about where to stay in Bath and decide where you would stay and why.

 Where to Stay in Bath

The Bell and Dragon

The Bell and Dragon is a lively pub, conveniently situated just ten minutes' walk from the city centre. It has 8 guest rooms and a large car park. Breakfast and evening meals are served in the dining room or guests can enjoy a drink and a snack in the main bar, which has a selection of fine ales, a dartboard and regular Friday quiz nights.

Bed and Breakfast

There are several bed and breakfast establishments throughout the city, where you can get a room with breakfast for a reasonable price. Try Mrs Baxter at 9 Mews Street or Mr and Mrs Jenkins at 13 Victoria Crescent.

2

You are going to read a story by the British author Roald Dahl about a seventeen-year-old boy called Billy. He arrives in Bath to start a new job, and needs to find somewhere to stay. Where do you think Billy would stay? Read the first part of the story.

The Landlady

Billy Weaver had travelled down from London on the slow afternoon train, and by the time he got to Bath it was about nine o'clock in the evening and the moon was coming up out of a clear starry sky over the houses opposite the station entrance.

'Excuse me,' he said, 'but is there a fairly cheap hotel near here?'

'Try the Bell and Dragon,' the porter answered, pointing down the road. 'They might have rooms. It's about a quarter of a mile from here.'

Billy thanked him, picked up his suitcase and set out to walk to the Bell and Dragon. He had never been to Bath before. He didn't know anyone who lived there. But Mr Greensale at the Head Office in London had told him it was a splendid city. 'Find your own lodgings,' he had said, 'then go along and report to the Branch Manager as soon as you're settled.'

Billy was seventeen years old. He was wearing a new navy-blue overcoat, a new brown hat, and a new brown suit, and he was feeling fine.

There were no shops on this wide street he was walking along, only a line of tall houses on each side, all of them identical. They had porches and pillars and four or five steps going up to their front doors, and it was obvious that once they had been very smart residences. But now, even in the darkness, he could see that the paint was peeling from the woodwork of their doors and windows, and that the handsome facades were cracked from neglect.

Suddenly, in a downstairs window that was brilliantly illuminated by a street-lamp, Billy saw a notice propped up against the glass. It said BED AND BREAKFAST.

He stopped walking, He moved a bit closer. Green curtains were hanging down on either side of the window. He went right up and peered through the glass into the room, and the first thing he saw was a bright fire burning in the hearth. On the carpet in front of the fire, a pretty little dachshund was curled up asleep with its nose tucked into its belly. The room itself, as far as he could see in the half-darkness, was filled with furniture. There was a baby-grand piano and a big sofa and several plump armchairs; and in one corner he spotted a parrot in a cage. Animals were usually a good sign in a place like this, Billy told himself; and all in all, it looked to him as though it would be a pretty decent house to stay in. Certainly it would be cosier than the Bell and Dragon.

On the other hand, a pub would be more lively than a bed and breakfast. There would be beer and darts in the evening and lots of people to talk to, and it would probably be cheaper, too. He had stayed a couple of nights in a pub once before and he had liked it.

UNIT 3 LESSON 1

3

Find the following words in the text. Try to guess the meaning of the words from the context.

1 porch _____
2 hearth _____
3 dachshund _____
4 cosy _____
5 darts _____

Use a dictionary to check.

4

The following phrases describe what happens in the next part of the story. In pairs, decide what you think happens to Billy.

a a queer thing happened to him
b he couldn't look away
c forcing him to stay where he was
d reaching for the bell

[cassette] Compare your ideas with another pair, and then listen to the next part of the story.

5

Read the conversation between Billy and the landlady of the bed and breakfast. Fill the gaps with six of the words in the box.

> advice   charge   cheap   knew   increase
> notice   ready   reduce   take

'I saw the _____ in the window,' he said, nervously.

'Yes, I know.'

'I was wondering about a room.'

'It's all _____ for you, my dear,' she said. She had a round pink face and very gentle blue eyes.

'I was on my way to the Bell and Dragon,' Billy told her. 'But the notice in your window just happened to catch my eye.'

'My dear boy,' she said, 'why don't you come in out of the cold?'

'How much do you _____?'

'Five and sixpence a night, including breakfast.'

It was fantastically _____ . It was less than half of what he had been willing to pay.

'If that is too much,' she added, 'then perhaps I can _____ it just a tiny bit. Do you want an egg for breakfast? Eggs are expensive at the moment. It would be sixpence less without the egg.'

'Five and sixpence is fine,' he answered. 'I should like very much to stay here.'

'I _____ you would. Do come in.'

6

Before you listen to the next part of the story, try to answer these questions.

1 Are there any hats and coats in the hall?
2 Are there a lot of guests at the bed and breakfast?
3 What reason does the landlady give for rejecting the other guests?
4 Why does the landlady say that Billy is 'exactly right'?

[cassette] Now listen and find out what happens.

Homework

Write a description of the landlady, so that someone who had not read the story would have a clear picture of what she is like. What is her face like? What kind of clothes does she wear?

Language Summary

Order of adjectives
   He was wearing a **new navy-blue** overcoat.
   She had a **round pink** face and **very gentle blue** eyes.

Subclauses without verbs
   Situated near the Royal Crescent, it offers comfortable, quiet accommodation.

see practice page 72

Unit 3 A place to stay

Lesson 2 'I'll give you a nice cup of tea ...'

Language focus: Question tags
Intensifiers: *so, such, do*

Skills focus: Speaking: Predicting
Reading and listening for specific information

1

Work in pairs. Here are some objects from the story. Some are from Lesson 1 and some are from this lesson. What are the objects and what part do you think they will play in the story?

2

 Listen to the next part of the story and then answer the questions.

1 What shows that the landlady had been expecting a visitor?
2 Why does Billy want to go to bed early?
3 What is the book the landlady wants Billy to sign?
4 What is Billy's explanation for the landlady's strange behaviour?

3

Work in pairs and discuss what you think is going to happen next. Then read the next part of the story to see if you are correct.

A few minutes later, after unpacking his suitcase and washing his hands, he went downstairs to the ground floor and entered the living-room. His landlady wasn't there, but the fire was glowing in the hearth, and the little dachshund was still sleeping in front of it. The room was wonderfully warm and cosy. I'm a lucky fellow, he thought, rubbing his hands.

He found the visitors' book lying open on the piano, so he took out his pen and wrote down his name and address. There were only two other entries above his on the page, and he started to read them. One was Christopher Mulholland from Cardiff. The other was Gregory W. Temple from Bristol.

That's funny, he thought suddenly. Christopher Mulholland. It rings a bell. Now where on earth had he heard that rather unusual name before? Was he a boy at school? No. Was it one of his sister's numerous boyfriends, perhaps, or a friend of his father's? No, no, it wasn't any of those. He glanced down again at the book.

Christopher Mulholland   231 Cathedral Road, Cardiff
Gregory W. Temple   27 Sycamore Drive, Bristol

As a matter of fact, now he came to think of it, the second name seemed very familiar too.

'Gregory Temple,' he said aloud, searching his memory. 'Christopher Mulholland ...'

4

Match the words on the left with the correct definitions on the right.

1 to glow   a to have a quick look
2 to ring a bell   b wherever
3 where on earth   c to burn red without
4 to glance   a flame
                       d to remind someone of
                         something

UNIT 3 LESSON 2

5

What is strange about the number of entries in the guest book and the names written there? In pairs discuss why Billy might recognise the names.

6

Look at these sentences, which come from the next part of the story. Who do you think says each one, Billy or the landlady? Write B or L in the box.

1 'Such charming boys.'
2 'The names sound somehow familiar.'
3 'Oh, no, I don't think they were famous.'
4 'They were tall and young and handsome, my dear, just exactly like you.'
5 'This last entry is over two years old.'
6 'How time flies, doesn't it?'
7 'In one ear and out the other, that's me.'

 Now listen to the next part of the story and check your answers.

7

Work in pairs. Try to remember if the following statements about the last part of the story you heard are true or false. If they are false, correct them.

Then listen again and check.

1 Billy knows that the boys were famous cricketers or footballers.
2 Both boys were good-looking.
3 The last entry in the guest book was quite recent.
4 Christopher Mulholland's entry is the last one in the book.
5 The landlady is bad at remembering names.

8

Read the next part of the story and answer the questions.

1 What does Billy find extraordinary?
2 How does the landlady react to what Billy says about the names?
3 What does Billy notice while the landlady is getting tea ready?

Write the first two paragraphs of the news article that would go with the headline you chose.

'You know something?' Billy said. 'Something that's really quite extraordinary about all this?'

'No, dear, I don't.'

'Well, you see – both of these names, Mulholland and Temple, I not only seem to remember each one of them separately, so to speak, but somehow or other, they both appear to be connected together. As though they were both famous for the same sort of thing, if you see what I mean – like … Churchill and Roosevelt.'

'How amusing,' she said. 'But come over here now, dear, and sit down beside me on the sofa and I'll give you a nice cup of tea and a ginger biscuit before you go to bed.'

'You really shouldn't bother,' Billy said. 'I didn't mean you to do anything like that.' He stood by the piano, watching her as she fussed about with the cups and saucers. He noticed that she had small, white, quickly-moving hands, and red fingernails.

'I'm almost positive it was in the newspapers I saw them,' Billy said. 'I'll think of it in a second. I'm sure I will.'

9

Billy thinks he might have read about Mr Mulholland and Mr Temple in the newspapers. With a partner, choose one of the headlines and discuss what you think the newspaper story is about.

Mystery of second missing teenager

Schoolboy friends in World Cup team

Boy saves old lady from fire horror

Mulholland and Temple still missing – search continues

Language Summary

Question tags
  It is Mr Perkins, **isn't it?**
  They weren't famous in any way, **were they?**
  How time flies, **doesn't it?**

Intensifiers
  I'm **so** glad you appeared.
  Such charming boys.
  I **do** apologise.

see practice page 73

Unit 3 A place to stay

Lesson 3 'The perfect age!'

Language focus: Short answers: *so am I, neither do I*
Adverbials; modifications of degree

Skills focus: Reading and listening for specific information; predicting

1

Look at the photographs and the headline from the newspaper, which Billy thinks he remembers. Discuss in groups where you think the two boys are.

First Mulholland, now Temple – where are they?

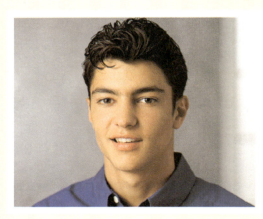

2

Read the next part of the story and find the word in the text that means:

1 sure
2 a student at university
3 to touch with your hand

'I'm almost positive it was in the newspapers I saw them,' Billy said. 'I'll think of it in a second. I'm sure I will.'

Billy frowned as he tried to remember.

'Now wait a minute,' he said. 'Wait just a minute. Mulholland … Christopher Mulholland … wasn't that the name of the schoolboy who was on a walking-tour through the West Country, near Bath, and then all of a sudden …'

'Milk?' she said. 'And sugar?'

'Yes, please. And then all of a sudden …'

'Schoolboy?' she said. 'Oh, no, my dear, that can't possibly be right because *my* Mr Mulholland was certainly not a schoolboy when he came to me. He was an undergraduate. Come over here now and sit next to me and warm yourself in front of this lovely fire. Come on. Your tea's all ready for you.' She patted the empty place beside her on the sofa, and she sat there smiling at Billy and waiting for him to come over.

3

Billy is beginning to feel uncomfortable. Why do you think this is? Underline the words in the text which show how the landlady is trying to make him feel more comfortable.

UNIT 3 LESSON 3

4

The landlady says something surprising in the next part of the story. In pairs, discuss what you think she is going to say.

 Now listen to the next part of the story. Were you right?

5

In the next part of the story, the landlady remembers various facts about Mr Mulholland and Mr Temple. Before reading the text, discuss in pairs which of the following points you would expect a landlady to remember about a previous guest.

1 his personality
2 his general appearance
3 whether he kept his room tidy or not
4 the colour of his teeth
5 what his skin was like

> Billy set down his cup slowly on the table, and stared at his landlady. She smiled back at him, and then she put out one of her white hands and patted him comfortingly on the knee. 'How old are you, my dear?' she asked.
>
> 'Seventeen.'
>
> 'Seventeen!' she cried. 'Oh, it's the perfect age! Mr Mulholland was also seventeen. But I think he was a trifle shorter than you are, in fact I'm sure he was, and his teeth weren't *quite* so white. You have the most beautiful teeth, Mr Weaver, did you know that?'
>
> 'They're not as good as they look,' Billy said. 'They've got simply masses of fillings in them at the back.'
>
> 'Mr Temple, of course, was a little older,' she said, ignoring his remark. 'He was actually twenty-eight. And yet I never would have guessed it if he hadn't told me, never in my whole life. There wasn't a mark on his body.'
>
> 'A what?' Billy said.
>
> 'His skin was just like a baby's.'

Now compare what you had expected the landlady to remember with what the landlady said. Were you surprised by anything?

6

The following things happen in the next part of the story. Put them in the order you think they will happen. Number them 1–6.

a Billy realises something about the dachshund. ☐
b Billy notices something about his drink. ☐
c The landlady is quiet for some time. ☐
d The landlady has difficulty in remembering one of the names. ☐
e The landlady explains how many guests she has had in the last two or three years. ☐
f Billy makes a comment about the parrot. ☐

 Now listen to the tape to check the order in which they happened.

7

Work in pairs and complete the sentences.

1 Billy thought that the parrot and the dachshund _____

2 The landlady explained that all her pets _____

3 Billy didn't really like the tea because _____

4 The landlady made sure that Billy had signed the guest book because _____

5 The only other guest that the landlady has had in the last two or three years _____

 Now listen again and check.

8

This is the end of the story. Discuss in groups what do you think will happen to Billy now.

> **Language Summary**
>
> Short answers
>   I'm looking for somewhere to stay.
>   **So am I.**
>   I don't want to stay in a hotel.
>   **Neither do I.**
>
> Adverbials: modifications of degree
>   I suppose he left **fairly** recently.
>
> **see practice page 74**

Write a different ending to the story.

Unit 4 Legends and heroes

Lesson 1 '... and they lived happily ever after'

Language focus: Past simple and past perfect
Narrative time markers

Skills focus: Speaking: storytelling
Reading and listening for gist
Writing a narrative composition

1

Find the definition of the word 'legend' in a dictionary. In small groups, tell the story of a well-known legend from your country. Is there any special message in the story? Does it teach people how they should behave? Does it have a happy ending, and is this important or not?

2

Look at the pictures, which show three legends. Which countries do you think the legends come from? What do you think the legends are about?

UNIT 4 LESSON 1

3

Below are the beginnings and endings of the three legends shown in the pictures. They are from China, Russia and Scandinavia. Read the legends and, in groups, match them to the pictures. Decide which legend comes from which country, and then discuss what you think happens in the middle of the legend.

A

A small group of people had been driven out of their valley by invaders, and forced to live in a dark forest. A young man called Danko had volunteered to lead them out of the forest to a new land, but the journey seemed hard and endless …

Everyone was so busy celebrating that they failed to notice that Danko was dead on the ground, with his heart lying beside him.

B

Once upon a time, a very rich, important official had a beautiful daughter called Koon-se. She fell in love with a poor shepherd called Chang, which made her father furious …

Koon-se prayed to the goddess Kwan-yin, who took pity on the pair and changed them into bluebirds, and they flew into the sky, free and together.

C

A beautiful young woman called Idun lived with the gods in Asgard, and was guardian of the golden apples, which they ate to keep their eternal youth. One day, Thizi, the storm god, captured Loki, the fire god, and demanded to be given Idun and the golden apples in exchange for Loki's freedom …

The gods were delighted to see Idun again, and the golden apples quickly restored their youth.

Write out your legend. Begin your legend with
Once upon a time …

4

Form new groups, and compare ideas for the middle part of each legend. Decide on the best ideas for each legend, and note them down.

 Listen to the complete legends. Compare the real stories with your ideas.

5

Do any of these legends have a message? If so, what do you think it is?

6

 Look at these words and phrases. Can you remember which of the legends they came from? Listen to the legends again and check.

> blamed   disguised   eternal youth
> forest   guards   magical powers   shepherd
> thunderstorm   took pity   transformed

7

In pairs, invent your own legend. You will need to consider the following questions:

When and where does the story take place?
Is there a message to the legend?
Who were the main characters?
What happened to them?
What was the central part of the legend?
If there was a problem, how was it resolved?
What kind of ending should the legend have?

Language Summary

Past simple and past perfect
  Danko **had volunteered** to lead them out of the forest … but the journey **seemed** hard and endless.

Narrative time markers
  Once upon a time a very rich, important official had a beautiful daughter called Koon-se.

see practice page 75

Unit 4 Legends and heroes

Lesson 2 *Robbing the rich to give to the poor*

Language focus: *Used to* and past simple
Used to and *would*

Skills focus: Reading: ordering a text; completing a text
Listening for main ideas

1

Look at the photograph. Work in pairs. Do you know who this person is? Can you name any famous folk heroes in your country? What were they famous for? What happened to them in the end?

2

The following text is about Robin Hood, an English folk hero, who is also well-known internationally. Put sentences in the correct order. Number them 1 to 6.

a Another character supplies the romantic interest in the legend. When people speak of Robin Hood, they always mention Maid Marian, the brave and beautiful woman who helped him defeat his enemies.

b People all over the world know his name, and know that he used to rob the rich to give to the poor.

c One of the most famous folk heroes of all time is Robin Hood.

d He used to do this by surprising rich travellers in Sherwood Forest, where he had his camp, out of reach of his enemy, the Sheriff of Nottingham.

e According to tradition, as he lay dying, Robin shot an arrow into the forest and asked to be buried where it fell. Visitors to the forest today can see a memorial stone which marks the place where he is supposed to be buried.

f Living in the forest with him were many other famous characters, such as Little John, Will Scarlet, Friar Tuck and Alan A'Dale.

UNIT 4 LESSON 2

3

In Nottingham there is an exhibition centre called 'The Tales of Robin Hood'. Visitors can see different scenes from the legend brought vividly to life. Listen to Rod and Debbie talking about their visit to the exhibition and answer these questions.

1 What did Debbie find most interesting?
2 What was most surprising about their visit?

4

Read the descriptions of some of the scenes at the exhibition. In pairs, choose a heading for each section and complete the text with phrases from the lists below.

Headings
The Feast
The Adventure Begins
Tradespeople
The Royal Forests

Phrases
a were corrupt and all were hated
b has one of the oldest professions in practice today
c working in the Middle Ages
d is the most virtuous and noble man in the world
e who robbed the rich to give to the poor

A _____
The story of our outlaw, (1) _____, has been recreated in three dimensions. Not just in sight, but in sound, smell and atmosphere. Welcome to the world of Robin Hood.

B _____
It was not unusual to find women (2) _____, especially if it was the family trade. Eleanor is seen hanging dyed wool cloth out to dry. Beside her are buckets full of dye and baskets of wool ready for dyeing.
The blacksmith (3) _____. Techniques haven't changed very much since people started working in iron, and they have hardly changed at all since the 13th century. Our blacksmith's workshop is almost identical to the ones you can see today.

C _____
They did not just provide the King with sport, but also with a lot of money from rents and payments for special privileges, from fines and from the sale of forest products. The forests also provided food for the king and his followers. Forest officials were employed to make sure the forest law was kept. Many (4) _____.
It is not surprising that people loved stories of Robin killing the King's deer.

D _____
A rich man sits next to Friar Tuck. You can also see Maid Marian and Robin himself, who is proposing a toast to the King sitting at the head of the table. The King (5) _____ in Robin's eyes. The King is surprised, however, by the fact that Robin is leaping on the table to toast him in his presence, something that is not normally allowed.

5

In the same pairs, discuss how you would design a poster to advertise the exhibition centre. Think of a heading for the poster which would attract visitors to the centre. What other information will you need to put on the poster?

Language Summary

Used to and past simple
  He **used to** rob the rich to give to the poor.
  Robin **shot** an arrow into the forest and **asked** to be buried where it **fell**.

Used to and *would*
  The most interesting part was seeing how people **used to** live.
  What they **used to/would** eat.

see practice page 76

Make the poster you planned in Activity 5.

Unit 4 Legends and heroes

Lesson 3 *The girl who heard voices*

Language focus: Impersonal passive

Skills focus: Listening for specific information
Speaking: making a radio programme

1

How much do you know about Joan of Arc? Circle the answers you think are correct and then check them in pairs.

1 Joan of Arc was:
   a) Belgian   b) English   c) French

2 She was born in:
   a) 1412   b) 1512   c) 1612

3 When she died she was:
   a) 9   b) 19   c) 90

4 She is famous for being a:
   a) writer   b) sailor   c) soldier

5 She helped to liberate the city of:
   a) Brussels   b) Paris   c) Orléans

 Listen to the tape, and check your answers.

2

 Listen again to the account of Joan's life, and answer the questions below.

1 What did the voices tell Joan to do?
2 Which army had surrounded Orléans?
3 What happened at Compiègne in 1430?
4 Why was Joan killed?
5 What happened five hundred years after Joan's death?
6 What can be seen in Orléans today in memory of Joan?

UNIT 4 LESSON 3

3

Work in groups and use the pictures to retell the story of Joan of Arc.

4

Imagine that your group has been given two minutes on a radio history programme for schools to tell the story of Joan of Arc. Discuss what you are going to say to make the story come alive for children. What sound effects will you have? Will you have any music? Record your story on a cassette-recorder, or write the script on a large card.

5

Listen to all the tape-recordings, or display the scripts, and choose the most effective one, giving the reasons for your choice.

6

Work in pairs. Tell your partner who is the most famous historical character in your country. What did this person do and why are they remembered?

Language Summary

Impersonal passive

It is believed that she led the French army to free the city of Orléans from the English.
She is believed to have led the French army to free the city of Orléans from the English.
It was said that Joan of Arc was a witch.
Joan of Arc **was said** to have been a witch.

see practice page 77

Homework

Write a paragraph about the most famous historical character in your country.

Unit 5 Fire and theft

Lesson 1 *The work of a moment*

Language focus: Reported speech; changes to the verb
Temporal changes to words
Skills focus: Listening for main ideas and detail
Writing: taking notes

1

Look at the three headlines from three different newspapers about one incident. In groups of three discuss what you think happened. Then compare your ideas with another group.

MYSTERY HERO CHASES THIEF

DARING RAID AT BANK

BANK ROBBER SNATCHES £500

2

 Listen to a radio report of the bank raid and see if your predictions were correct.

3

In pairs, using what you know from the radio report, correct the five mistakes in this newspaper report of the incident.

 Then listen again and check your answers.

A daring bank robber got away with about £700 in a raid on a bank in Peterston yesterday. The incident happened just after midday at the Westland Bank in the High Street.

According to the police, the man went up to the desk and asked the bank clerk to exchange ten pound coins for a £10 note. As she was changing the money, he reached over and put his hand into the drawer. The bank clerk, Valerie Simpson, bravely tried to trap his fingers in the drawer, but he managed to grab the money and run away.

A passer-by, who has not been identified, chased the man down the street and recovered some of the money which he had dropped, but the thief then disappeared into a crowded supermarket.

Eyewitnesses described the thief as being middle-aged, about 1·78 metres tall, slim, with short brown hair and with a pale complexion. He was wearing a blue lightweight jacket.

4

Read the newspaper report again and find all the words that you can use to talk about crime. Put them in the correct columns below. Then add any other words you can think of.

Verbs	Adjectives	Nouns
to get away	daring	bank robber

UNIT **5** LESSON **1**

5

How accurately would you be able to describe a thief if you were an eyewitness to a crime? Work with a partner. One of you look at Picture A and the other look at Picture B. You have thirty seconds to look at your picture.

Close your books. Take turns being a police officer interviewing an eyewitness. The eyewitness must tell the police officer as many details about the thief as they can remember. The police officer must make notes about what the eyewitness says. Then change roles.

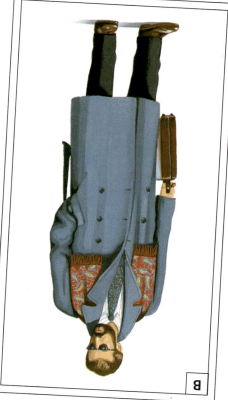

6

Now compare the notes you have made with the pictures. Which one of you was the better eyewitness?

7

With your partner, choose one of the pictures and decide what crime the person has committed. Make notes about the crime using these questions to help you.

Where did the incident take place?
What time was it?
What happened?
Were there any eyewitnesses?
Did anyone try to stop the criminal?
Did he run away or did he have a car?
Have the police caught the criminal?

Using the notes you made in Activity 7, write a short report of your crime. You can also use the newspaper report about the Westland Bank robbery as a model.

Language Summary

Reported speech: changes to the verb
'I **am** still a bit shocked' Valerie said.
Valerie said that she **was** a bit shocked.
'What time **did** the robbery **happen**?' asked the reporter.
The reporter asked what time the robbery **had happened**.

Temporal changes to words
'I'm standing outside the Westland Bank where the raid took place **this** morning' said the reporter.
The reporter said that he was standing outside the Westland Bank where the raid had taken place **that** morning.

see practice page 78

Unit 5 Fire and theft

Lesson 2 *A puff of smoke*

Language focus: Reported speech: questions
Reporting verbs

Skills focus: Listening for main ideas; note-taking
Speaking: roleplaying a conversation

1

Work in pairs. Think of as many jobs as you can that you would classify as dangerous. What do you think are the advantages and disadvantages of these jobs? What kind of qualities do you need to do them?

2

Josie Lucas is a firefighter. You are going to listen to her talking about her job. Write five questions about her job that you would like her to answer.

3

Now listen to the interview. Were your questions answered?

4

Try to remember what Josie said and make notes to complete the table. Did she mention any of the points you noted in Activity 1?

qualities needed	
advantages of the job	
disadvantages of the job	

5

Listen to Josie talking about an incident she was involved in. As you listen, make notes about these things:
– what happened at the warehouse
– what Josie did
– what she could see and feel
– what happened at the end
– what Josie's husband was doing

UNIT 5 LESSON 2

6

Josie used all these two-part verbs to tell the story of the warehouse fire. Can you remember what she said? Check the meanings in a dictionary.

> catch hold   climb into   get out   go off (2)
> put out   rush in   rush off   tune in

Use the two-part verbs (in the correct tense) to fill in the gaps in these sentences.

1 The alarm _____ and the firefighters _____ the fire engine.

2 Josie's husband _____ to the radio to find out where she was.

3 When they heard the alarm, the firefighters _____ to the scene of the fire.

4 The gas cylinders _____ like firecrackers.

5 The firefighters managed to _____ the fire.

6 When the doors were opened and air _____, the fire _____ and spread rapidly.

7 When the building started to collapse, the firefighters had to _____ as quickly as possible.

7

Work in pairs. Listen to Josie again, and make notes on the different attitudes of Josie and her husband to the situation. One of you make notes about Josie, the other about her husband.

8

With your partner act out the conversation between Josie and her husband when she gets home from work.

Josie
Try to explain to your husband why you didn't phone him after the warehouse fire.

Husband
Try to explain to Josie how you feel when she is at a dangerous fire and why you would like her to phone you afterwards.

Homework

Write a short report about the warehouse fire. Use the notes you made in Activity 5 and these questions to help you.

Where was the fire?
What did the firefighters do?
Why couldn't they stay in the building?
What happened when they opened the doors of the warehouse?
Why was the fire so noisy?
Were the firefighters successful in putting out the fire?
Was there a lot of damage?

Language Summary

Reported speech: questions
  '**Do you** ever **regret** changing your job, Josie?' asked the reporter.
  The reporter asked Josie **if/whether she** ever **regretted** changing her job.

Reporting verbs
  'I'm sorry I didn't phone you', said Josie.
  Josie **apologised for** not **phoning**.

see practice page 79

Unit 5 Fire and theft

Lesson 3 *A crime or a joke?*

Language focus: Definite, indefinite and zero articles
Skills focus: Listening and reading to order and complete a text

1

Look at this photograph and the newspaper headline. In pairs discuss what you think the newspaper story is about.

2

Listen to a newspaper reporter interviewing Tina Davies and see if your predictions were correct.

3

Using what you have heard, put this newspaper report in the correct order and fill in the missing words.

Then listen again to check.

EXCLUSIVE

GORDON THE GNOME BACK FROM HIS HOLIDAYS

☐ Gordon's holiday took him to France, Sweden, Germany, Japan, Italy, New Zealand, Mexico, Brazil, Ireland, Spain, Austria and _____. Gordon the Gnome disappeared from Tina Davies's front garden last spring. There had been a number of thefts of gnomes in the area, but the police were unable to find the _____.

☐ Over the next few months, Tina received 12 postcards, each from a different country, and each showing Gordon enjoying his holiday – on beaches, in bars, at the Pyramids, even skiing!

☐ A few weeks later, Tina got her first postcard from Gordon. It showed the gnome on a beach with a suitcase and it was sent from _____. The postcard said, 'Having a wonderful time, Gordon'.

☐ Then one day he turned up back home on the doorstep, with his _____ and a note to say that he was happy to be home.

☐ Tina showed the postcard to the police, but they laughed and said it must be someone in the family playing a _____ on her, someone who knew that the gnome's name was Gordon. However, Tina couldn't think of anyone who could be doing this and she didn't know anyone in France.

UNIT 5 LESSON 3

4

At first Tina thought that children had taken Gordon from the garden. What did she tell the reporter that the children in the area had done with other people's gnomes?

5

Discuss in pairs: Was Gordon's disappearance a joke or a crime?

6

Read this sentence from the article again.

There had been a number of *thefts* of gnomes in the area, but police were unable to find the *thief*.

Now complete this table with the names of crimes or criminals.

	Crime	Criminal
1	*theft*	thief
2	murder	
3	arson	
4		vandal
5	blackmail	
6	burglary	
7		shop-lifter
8	forgery	

Homework

Imagine you are Gordon the Gnome. Write a paragraph describing your travels. What was your favourite place, and why?

7

Look at this list of definitions of crimes. Match each one with one of the crimes in the table in Activity 6.

a breaking into people's houses and stealing things
b making false documents or printing fake money
c setting fire to buildings
d damaging buildings or property
e taking things from shops without paying
f threatening to reveal a person's secrets unless they give you money
g taking something that belongs to someone else
h killing someone

8

In groups decide which of the crimes in Activity 6 you think is the most serious. Number them 1 to 8 with 1 being the most serious and 8 the least serious. Then compare your list with another group.

Language Summary

The definite article
   There had been a number of thefts in **the** area.
   Then **the** first postcard arrived.

The indefinite article
   We got **a** postcard from France.
   A police officer has to wear **a** uniform.

Zero article
   Crime doesn't pay.
   Children often play jokes on people.

see practice page 80

Unit 6 Have you got a problem?

Lesson 1 *Strange obsessions*

Language focus: Relative pronouns
Relative clauses

Skills focus: Reading for specific information
Listening to complete a table

1

Work in pairs. Do you collect things? Do you know anyone who collects any of the things below? Tell your partner about them.

> autographs   badges and stickers   coins
> football cards   postcards   photographs   stamps

2

Look at the photograph of Mel Watson, who collects pineapple-shaped objects. How many different objects can you see? What do you think some of them might be?

3

Now read the text, and find the answers to these questions.

1. How did Mel's pineapple collection start?
2. How many pineapples has she got?
3. Which is her favourite pineapple object?
4. Does she like eating pineapples?

> Mel Watson collects pineapples. Ten years ago, some friends gave her a plastic ice bucket in the shape of a pineapple and since then her collection has grown to over 100 objects, all in the shape of or decorated with pineapples.
>
> 'It all started with that ice bucket,' Mel says. 'Once you've got one thing that is pineapple-shaped, people just keep giving you more – for birthdays, for Christmas, souvenirs from holidays, nothing but pineapples! I didn't deliberately set out to collect pineapples, it just happened. And once I had three or four things, I started to become interested in the number of objects that you can get connected with pineapples and I started buying them for myself. You would be surprised just how many things are made in the shape of pineapples. I've got china mugs, plates, scissors, glass jars, place mats, wooden napkin rings, fridge magnets, a soapdish, a cutting board, a lamp, a fan, earrings … and then there are the things which have pictures of pineapples on them – paintings, linen tablecloths, aprons, teatowels, T-shirts …'
>
> So where does she keep her collection?
>
> 'In the kitchen. I don't think I could bear to have the whole house covered in pineapples! I keep them in the kitchen – and I have pineapple wallpaper in the kitchen as well.'
>
> Mel's favourite pineapple object is a beautiful pineapple brooch which her brother bought for her in France. The most unusual is a pair of plastic pineapples from Japan which can be used for massaging hands.
>
> And does Mel like eating pineapples?
>
> 'Yes, I do. But then I suppose I would have to say that, wouldn't I?'

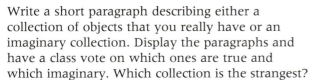

Homework

Write a short paragraph describing either a collection of objects that you really have or an imaginary collection. Display the paragraphs and have a class vote on which ones are true and which imaginary. Which collection is the strangest?

4

Read the passage again and underline five adjectives that tell you what the objects are made from. How many other adjectives can you add to this list?

5

In pairs discuss how many of the objects Mel mentions are useful and how many are just decorative.

6

Listen to Kate and Jim talking about other people who collect things. As you listen fill in the table.

Name	What he collects	Where he is from	How many he has got
Bill McDaniel			
			7,445
Teiichi Yoshizawa			
R Jones			
		Santa Clara, California	

Listen again and check your answers.

7

In pairs discuss which collection you think is the strangest. Could you ever become an obsessive collector, and if so, what would you want to collect?

Language Summary

Relative pronouns
  There are many things **which/that** have pineapples on them.
  Someone **who** collects ties is called a grabatologist.
  I have a friend **whose** kitchen is full of pineapples.

Defining relative clauses
  It's all about a Japanese man **who collects matchbox labels**.

Non-defining relative clauses
  Bill McDaniel, **who lives in California**, collects ties.

see practice page 81

Unit 6 Have you got a problem?

Lesson 2 *To buy or not to buy?*

Language focus: Ways of giving advice

Skills focus: Reading a questionnaire; for gist
Listening: inferring

1

Work in pairs. Look at the picture. Describe what the woman looks like, how she feels and what she is thinking about.

2

Answer the questionnaire below.

3

In pairs, compare your scores. Do you believe this assessment? Do you enjoy shopping? Do you find shopping difficult or easy?

Are YOU a compulsive shopper?

Score: Strongly agree 5; agree 4; neither agree nor disagree 3; disagree 2; strongly disagree 1.

1. Sometimes I feel that something inside pushes me to go shopping.
2. There are times when I have a strong urge to buy things (clothing, tapes, jewellery, etc.).
3. There are things I buy that I do not show to anybody for fear they will think I've done something stupid or wasted my money.
4. I often have a spontaneous desire to buy something.
5. As soon as I enter a shopping centre, I have an irresistible urge to buy something.
6. I have often bought a product that I didn't need, even when I knew I have very little money.
7. When feeling depressed I have to buy something.
8. When using my credit card I often don't have enough money available in the bank.

Under 10 What a careful person you are!

10 to 33 You enjoy shopping, but you don't necessarily have a problem.

Over 35 You may be a compulsive shopper!

UNIT 6 LESSON 2

4

Read the text and match the paragraphs 1–7 to the summaries a–g below.

Summaries

a People who feel compelled to buy things often feel guilty afterwards.

b She is really addicted to shopping and is not just someone who buys things impulsively.

c She is compelled to behave compulsively to relieve her feelings, despite having a happy personal and professional life.

d People who buy compulsively tend not to unwrap what they've bought, as it is the actual act of purchase that gives them excitement.

e A survey into compulsive shopping was conducted.

f Compulsive shoppers' feelings vary from extreme happiness to absolute depression in a way which is similar to people with different addictions.

g The survey gave the researcher information about the age and income of compulsive shoppers and also the frequency of this behaviour.

1 Joanne is happily married and has a good job as a personal assistant. But several times a week she has a compulsive desire to indulge an addiction that not even her husband knows about. Just the thought of relief lifts her, but the high lasts only a few hours.

2 The first British research into the life of the shopping addict has revealed that the truly compulsive shopper is overcome by guilt and often hides or dumps the evidence after guilty spending sprees.

3 While many people experience pleasure at buying a new outfit or something for their children or home, the true shopping addict is trapped in a cycle of emotional highs and lows similar to drug addiction, alcoholism or compulsive gambling.

4 Marketing lecturer Dr Richard Elliott, of Lancaster University Management School, conducted in-depth interviews and gave an eight-page questionnaire to 52 people who identified themselves as addicted shoppers.

5 His results showed the typical British shopping addict to be aged 35–44. The largest group, nearly a third, had an average family income and more than half of them felt the urge to go shopping at least three times a week. One in five had to buy something every day.

6 Joanne is not simply an impulse shopper – everyone has given in to the occasional urge to spend. She is a true addict.

7 'The compulsive shopper buys three jumpers, or five pairs of shoes, but never even unwraps the purchases. Some compulsive shoppers have cupboards full of unopened parcels, others take their buys straight to the charity shop. The compulsive shopper is driven to buy to relieve depression and he or she gets a real thrill from the act of purchasing,' says researcher Andrew Crowther.

5

Listen to Dr Elliott, and in pairs decide whether he would agree with the following statements.

1 People who shop compulsively are rather like people who drink too much alcohol.
2 Compulsive shopping is sometimes a means of dealing with a difficult life.
3 The act of shopping can lead to a feeling of depression.
4 It's important for compulsive shoppers to buy a large amount of goods.
5 Credit cards should be more strictly controlled.
6 Cutting up your credit card will solve the problem of compulsive shopping.

6

Dr Elliott used all the words in Box A to talk about the problem of compulsive shopping. Match the words in Box A with synonyms in Box B.

A
buy   destroy   device
reply   credit card   deal

B
plastic   cut up   mechanism
cope   purchase   response

Homework

Write a letter to Joanne, giving her advice on her problem.

Language Summary

Ways of giving advice
   You **should** cut up your credit card.
   You **ought to** cut up your credit card.
   You**'d better** cut up your credit card.
   Why don't you cut up your credit card?
   I suggest you cut up your credit card.
   How about cutting up your credit card?

see practice page 82

Unit 6 Have you got a problem?

Lesson 3 Nothing but the truth

Language focus: First conditional
Second conditional

Skills focus: Reading for specific information
Speaking: roleplaying a court scene

1

Work in pairs. Look at the picture. What is happening? What would you do if you were the woman on the right?

2

How important is it to you to stick to your beliefs? Decide what you would do in the following situations. Then discuss your answers in pairs and see if you have any different responses.

1 You believe in racial equality. You are invited to a friend's house for a meal. Your friend's father starts telling racist jokes during the meal.

2 You are watching *Crimebusters,* a TV programme which reconstructs crimes to help solve them. The gunman in a bank robbery looks just like your best friend.

3 Your best friend tells you that she has worked out a fool-proof way of cheating in examinations that you will both have to take at the end of the year.

3

Read the following letter which Cynthia, the woman on the right in the picture, wrote to a magazine.

15th March 1995

Dear Sue,

1 Three years ago my husband, Bob, was made redundant and he couldn't find work for nearly two years. He wrote many application letters, attended scores of interviews, only to be rejected. He became very moody and depressed.

2 Then he found a job through a chance meeting in the pub. At first Bob was appointed office manager for a small engineering company, but within six months he had been promoted to sales director.

3 Jane, his boss, was supportive and she played a large part in helping Bob regain his confidence.

4 Then one afternoon, when I was shopping in a record store, I noticed a teenager slip a CD into his bag and then hurry towards the exit. I felt duty-bound to inform a shop assistant of what I'd seen.

5 The boy was arrested by a store detective and I was asked to make a statement. The manager said I'd probably be called to appear in court as a witness.

6 I went home feeling pleased at having done the right thing, but my feelings changed to dismay the following evening when Bob told me the boy was his employer's son, William.

7 His boss had given him what amounted to an ultimatum: Jane had made it clear that Bob's future with his company depended on me withdrawing my statement or, if I was called as a witness, telling the court that I had been mistaken.

8 William's lawyer intended to tell the court he had slipped the CD into his bag by accident ---- an excuse my evidence would contradict. Bob pleaded with me to go along with this, saying it was crazy to risk his future for the sake of a big store.

9 I was brought up to believe that honesty is important, and if I lied I would feel terrible.

10 But have I the right to ruin my husband's career for a principle?

Yours sincerely

Cynthia Dawson

UNIT 6 LESSON 3

4

Find the words in the passage which have the meanings given below.

a to lose your job (because the company cannot afford to employ you any longer) (paragraph 1)
b to be given a higher position at work (paragraph 2)
c to be under some kind of obligation to do something (paragraph 4)
d someone who actually saw the incident in question take place (paragraph 5)
e a strong feeling of sadness caused (here) by some unexpected news (paragraph 6)
f a warning that if you do not accept certain conditions, action will be taken against you (paragraph 7)
g to show that a previous statement cannot be true (paragraph 8)

5

Cynthia now has several possible courses of action. She can:

1 tell the truth no matter what the consequences are;
2 say she made a mistake and withdraw her statement;
3 tell a lie in court.

In small groups, discuss the advantages and disadvantages of each course of action.

6

Work in groups. You are now going to act out the scene in the court. Look at the characters involved, and think about the questions each character must answer. Choose one of the roles and act out the court case.

Cynthia
Do I tell the truth? Do I lie? If I lie, what do I say? How can I make people believe me?

William
Do I tell the truth? How can I face my parents? Do I lie? If I lie, what can I say so that people believe me and not Cynthia? What reason can I give for having the CD?

Prosecution lawyer
What questions should I ask William to show that his story is not true? What should I ask the store detective? How can I prove that William is lying?

William's lawyer
What questions should I ask Cynthia to shake her story? How can I make her change her story? Are there any parts of her story that are not logical? Does the store detective back up her story?

Store detective
Am I sure exactly what happened? Am I sure that Cynthia didn't make a mistake? Have I seen William before?

Store manager
Am I clear exactly what happened? Is the shop to blame in any way? Does my store detective need support?

Judge
Do I understand exactly what happened? Is everyone's story clear? Do I need to ask further questions? Who do I believe and why?

The jury
Who do you believe and why?

7

In groups, discuss the role play and the verdict. What do you think will happen to Bob, Cynthia, William and Jane now?

Language Summary

First conditional
    If Cynthia **tells** the truth, Bob **will lose** his job.
    If I **lie**, how **can** I make people believe me?

Second conditional
    If I **lied** under oath, I **would feel** terrible.
    If I **were** Cynthia, I **would tell** the truth.

see practice page 83

Homework

Look again at Cynthia's letter on page 40 and write a reply from the magazine, advising her on the best thing to do and giving her clear reasons. Use these expressions:

If I were you, I would ...
If that happened to me, I would ...
I think that you should ...

Unit 7 Deceits, tricks and blunders

Lesson 1 *Never trust a stranger*

Language focus: Present participles
Skills focus: Reading for main ideas; inferring
Listening: ordering events
Writing: descriptions

1

Look at the picture, and in pairs decide what the situation is. How would you feel if you were in this situation? What would you do?

2

Read the first part of the story and underline the words that tell you how Julia feels.

Julia sat in her Mini, drumming her fingers to the beat of the rain on the windows. Cars zipped by like torpedoes, their drivers gazing zombie-like at the road ahead. Every now and again Julia would wave her arms and mouth her plea: 'Help! I've broken down!' But the drivers simply ignored her.

'And next,' crackled a presenter from the worn-out radio, 'we've got cricket from sunny Australia.'

Oh great!, Julia muttered through gritted teeth. Just what a girl needs when her car has come to a halt five miles outside Ashford on a rainy Friday night.

'But first, a news flash,' said the presenter in his serious broadcaster voice.

'Motorists should be on their guard after a robbery took place in a quiet country lane near Ashford this afternoon. This is the third such incident in as many weeks ...'

Julia shivered. She didn't want to hear this now.

'Drivers are advised to keep doors and windows locked,' the presenter was saying, 'and to be very careful about talking to strangers in deserted areas. Don't trust anyone, listeners, that's the golden rule.'

Julia glanced out at the darkening sky. She was beginning to feel nervous. Perhaps she should give up waiting for someone to help her.

'Need a hand, love?'

She looked round with a start. Parked nearby was a garish van bearing the words, *Terry Wilkins Removals — No Job Too Small*. The man peering in through the car window was large and burly, a cigarette welded to his lips and a lurid tattoo decorating his forearm. He couldn't have looked less trustworthy if he'd tried. Instantly Julia flicked down the lock on the door.

3

In pairs, say what kind of person you think Julia is. Make notes on her situation and what you think she will do.

4

Listen to the next part of the story. Put these events into the correct order. Number them 1 to 5 and listen again to check your answers

a The Peugeot stopped.
b Terry drove back towards Julia.
c Terry went back to his van.
d Terry stopped his van.
e The young man took off his raincoat.

5

Match the words on the left with the definitions on the right.

1 to pull up   a speak softly
2 assistance   b quick
3 vaguely   c make disapproving noises
4 coyly   d without trust
5 suspiciously   e in a shy but rather sly way
6 swift   f stop
7 tut   g help
8 murmur   h with no real purpose

UNIT 7 LESSON 1

6

In pairs, write a short description of the two men. Would you trust either of them?

Which of the following words best describe Julia's feelings towards each man?

> cautious distrustful grateful relieved
> snobbish suspicious trusting wary

Why does she feel like this? Do you agree with her attitudes?

7

Read the next part of the story and answer these questions:

1 Why do you think that Julia is suspicious?
2 How do you feel about this man?

'Any luck?' asked Julia brightly, leaning on the side of the car. The man emerged from under the bonnet and sucked in his breath.

'It's no good,' he said, putting on his coat. 'We will have to find a garage. Hop in. I'll give you a lift.'

Julia shot him a wary look. 'Well, I don't know …'

The man smiled. 'You can trust me,' he said gently and reached in his pocket for the car keys. Then suddenly his face clouded and he began frantically searching every pocket with mounting irritation.

'I don't believe it. My keys! I must have dropped them.'

Julia narrowed her eyes a little. Then she bent down and studied the ground carefully.

'There's nothing down here,' she said with a note of suspicion. 'Are you sure you haven't got them?'

'Of course I'm sure!' The man looked insulted. He dropped to his knees and began patting the damp ground. 'Don't you believe me?'

Seeing his hurt expression, Julia smiled apologetically. 'I'm sorry. Of course I trust you.'

The man groaned and pointed to a grate in the gutter. 'They must have fallen down there when I took my coat off.'

'What shall we do?' asked Julia.

'I'll have to ring my wife and get her to bring the spare set. Did you notice a phone box nearby?'

Julia nodded. 'About half a mile back. I was going to go to ring for help, but I didn't fancy wandering around on my own.'

'I'll go,' he offered. 'You stay here and lock yourself in your car. These roads are so badly lit, you never know who might be lurking in the shadows …'

8

The following words come from the next part of the story. In pairs, discuss what you think will happen next.

> empty Mini speed uneasy

9

Read the next part of the story. In pairs, can you explain what has happened?

'People should look where they are going,' muttered Terry Wilkins, swerving to avoid a man in a raincoat. 'Now where is it?' He frowned as he tried to remember where he'd seen the woman.

Suddenly the thought of the man in the raincoat made him uneasy. Speeding up in spite of the rain, he headed down the lane the man had come out of.

It was pitch black. He pulled over. The Mini was still there, but it was empty. The young woman was nowhere to be seen …

10

Listen to the end of the story. Were you right?

Homework

Write a radio announcement warning drivers about Julia and the trick she plays. Describe Julia, the car she is now driving and the way she tricks people.

Language Summary

Present participles
'It's no good,' he said, **putting on** his coat.
Seeing his hurt expression, Julia smiled apologetically.

see practice page 84

Unit 7 Deceits, tricks and blunders

Lesson 2 *They all look the same*

Language focus: Third conditional
Should(n't) have

Skills focus: Reading: ordering a text; for specific information
Listening: taking notes

1

With a partner, look at this newspaper headline. What do you think the article might be about?

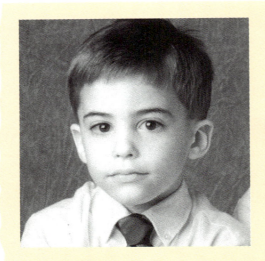

Mix-up at birth sets boys worlds apart

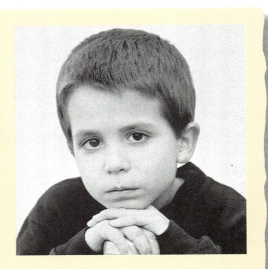

2

Now read part of the article. The paragraphs are in the wrong order. Put them in order, and see if your ideas about the article were correct.

1 The other, born to inherit wealth and privilege, lives only five miles away in a humble home with one small wage for the household each month.

2 The tragic mix-up was confirmed only days ago. Now the anguished couples in the case have taken the heart-breaking decision to leave the boys where they are and legally adopt the child they have been bringing up. This means that under German law the son born with a silver spoon in his mouth will lose his right to inherit from his real parents.

3 The mix-up, which happened six years ago when the boys were born within three days of each other in Wittmund, a small country town near Hamburg, was exposed by a former midwife at the clinic. The woman – now 71 and identified only as Maria·S. – said yesterday that the couples, who do not know each other, had spoken to her of their dilemma and their fears for the future.

4 Two children given to the wrong mothers in a maternity clinic muddle are growing up in startlingly different worlds, it emerged yesterday.

5 One of the boys, born to poor parents, is being brought up by a family of millionaires, with a large farmhouse and hundreds of acres of land.

UNIT 7 LESSON 2

3

Read the text again and answer the following questions.

1 When were the children mixed up?
2 How old are they now?
3 What have the parents decided to do?
4 Who let out the secret of the mix-up?
5 Describe the different lifestyles of the boys.

4

In pairs, discuss the following:

1 Why do you think the midwife decided to tell the truth?
2 What problems do you think the parents and children will face in the future?
3 What decisions will they all have to make?

5

Read the rest of the article, to see if your ideas agree with those in the newspaper.

'Perhaps one day, if the boys learn what happened, there will be envy … even hate,' she said. 'Perhaps the "poor" boy will say to himself, "All this could have belonged to me if the doctors hadn't made a mistake".'

'Both mothers, rich and poor, fear too that they will accidentally meet their real child. They dread the day when they might go into a supermarket and recognise their own flesh and blood,' said Maria.

(1) _____ It is assumed that one lost his tag and that a nurse gave him a new one with the wrong name.

Maria says she reported her suspicions to the clinic, but nobody believed her. (2) _____ Blood tests confirmed the mix-up, but a psychologist advised the families that another switch would be too great a shock for the children. It would be like losing their parents. (3) _____

But it is thought unlikely that in such a small community the secret can be kept.

Homework

Write a short summary of what you think the parents of the boys should do now. Give reasons for your opinion.

6

Put these sentences into the article in the correct places.

a For years, her conscience troubled her, and eventually she told the doctor of one of the families.
b Another warned that if the children ever learned the truth, they would undergo a severe identity crisis.
c She suspected that the babies had been muddled when both were found to be wearing the same name tag.

7

Listen to three people talking about the newspaper story. What do they say should be done in this situation? Make notes as you listen, and then compare your notes with a partner.

Robert	Sheila	Joanne

8

In groups, decide who gives the best advice for the parents of the two boys. If you disagree with them all, then suggest your own ideas.

Language Summary

Third conditional
   If the doctors **had believed** Maria's suspicions, there **wouldn't have been** the mix up.

Should(n't) have
   The doctors **should have** believed Maria.
   The doctors **shouldn't have** made a mistake.

see practice page 85

Unit 7 Deceits, tricks and blunders

Lesson 3 *Where there's smoke, there's fire*

Language focus: Revision of the passive: passive form of verbs
Passive form of modal verbs

Skills focus: Listening for gist
Reading for main ideas
Speaking: talking about urban myths

1

Look at the title of this lesson. What do you think it means? Which of the following is the best definition?

a Fires always smoke.
b You can't light a cigarette without a match.
c If lots of people talk about something, there must be some truth in what they say.

2

Listen to four people telling stories. Make notes about the stories. Do you believe them? Have you heard any of these stories before?

3

Stories like this are called 'urban myths'. They are often said to have happened to a distant relative or friend of the person telling the story. And yet the same stories are told all over the world. Look at the picture. In pairs, discuss what you think this story is about.

4

Now read the text below to check. What are the other three stories about?

1 He said it was the truth, he had heard it from someone who had actually been in the store at the time:

2 A woman went into the fashion department of a large Chicago store and tried on a coat. She put her hand in the pocket of the coat and was bitten by a snake. The coat had been made somewhere in South America and a viper had laid its eggs in the pocket.

3 There wasn't, of course, a word of truth in the story, but the same myth was soon being told in New York, Miami and Los Angeles, and over the past year it has crossed the Atlantic and back a few times. As a story – an urban myth – it is relatively harmless, except to the owners of the department store. However, the speed with which urban myths are passed on, the length of time they persist long after they have been shown to be untrue, and the effect they can sometimes have is now an issue of such concern that American social behaviour experts are seriously studying how they work.

4 Although it seems that people are more likely to believe the stories if they feature foreigners and unfamiliar settings, details of the stories are often changed to fit the place in which they are being told. The story of the London motorcyclist is a classic example. He was taking his driving test and the examiner was supposed to jump out and wave his hand to signal an emergency stop. The motorcyclist went round and round a roundabout until he ran out of petrol. Later he discovered that the examiner had jumped in front of the wrong motorcyclist and had ended up in hospital. This story, without authentication, actually appeared in a Florida newspaper as something that had happened in Fort Lauderdale.

UNIT 7 LESSON 3

5 Some urban myths can send the share dealings soaring or plunging in the City of London and on Wall Street because when the stories target companies, the impact can be devastating.

6 Dr James Bush, a social psychologist, advises major corporations on how to combat damaging stories. His prime objective is to kill a myth before it can get off the ground. The problem, however, is that people like these stories, and the more outrageous they are, the more likely they are to be repeated. Dr Bush interviews people who have heard the story, examines the evidence which is put forward to support it, and then devises a campaign to kill it dead.

7 Going the rounds last year was the story of the boy in a popular TV cereal advert. When the advert eventually came off the air, the story started to spread that the boy had mixed a fizzy drink with an exploding candy. The advert boy, it was alleged, died horribly. Sales of the fizzy drink fell dramatically and the company that made it brought in Dr Bush to try to save the situation.

8 When urban myths affect business they have to be stopped, and Dr Bush argues against the long-held public relations view that denials only call attention to the story. He claims that ignoring the stories rarely puts a stop to them and that it is better to make a public denial. But it is a tough decision for an executive to take.

9 Sales of a brand of bubblegum collapsed suddenly in New York after rumours swept every school playground that the bubblegum was made from spiders' eggs. The story was so outrageous that at first the company laughed it off, but sales of the bubblegum began to fall seriously all over the country as the story spread from state to state. Executives were so convinced that it was a myth spread by a rival company that they hired an army of private detectives. The detectives were baffled: 'It's a story and it's everywhere', they reported, but they couldn't find the source. In the end there had to be a public denial. When it was made, the story died, but by then it had done a lot of damage to the product.

5

Make notes under the following headings:

- Characteristics of urban myths
- Effects of urban myths on companies
- The psychologist's advice

6

Look back at the text and underline the adverbs of manner which tell you *how* something happened.

For example: *Sales fell dramatically.*

7

Find words or phrases in the text that mean:

1 to last (paragraph 3)
2 rising (paragraph 5)
3 falling (paragraph 5)
4 damaging (paragraph 5)
5 start (paragraph 6)
6 shocking (paragraph 6)
7 difficult (paragraph 8)
8 surprised (paragraph 9)
9 origin (paragraph 9)

8

In groups discuss the following questions.

1 Have you heard any of the stories in the text before?
2 Were the details different? If so, how?
3 Do you have any other urban myths like this in your country?

Language Summary

Revision of the passive: passive form of verbs
The coat **had been made** somewhere in South America.
The speed in which urban myths **are passed on** is an issue of concern.
Passive form of modal verbs
  Urban myths **mustn't be taken** too seriously.
  The story **might have been started** by rivals.

see practice page 86

Homework

Write an urban myth that you have heard or invent one of your own.

Unit 8 All in the mind

Lesson 1 *I think, therefore ...*

Language focus: Comparative forms of adjectives
Comparisons: equality and inequality
Comparisons: adverbs

Skills focus: Listening for main ideas
Reading and answering a quiz

1

Work in pairs. Look at these educational children's toys. Discuss what skills these toys can teach children. Which ones are suitable for very young children? Do you think any of the toys are more suitable for girls or more suitable for boys and why?

2

Look at this list of abilities and qualities. In groups decide whether you think men or women are better at the following things. Write M or F in the box.

singing in tune ☐	parking cars ☐
reading and spelling ☐	reading maps ☐
seeing in the dark ☐	concentration ☐
hand co-ordination ☐	sharp hearing ☐
good sense of smell ☐	logical ☐

3

Read the following text about differences between the sexes.

HOW THE SEXES GROW APART

It's often said that the differences between men and women are a result of the different ways they're brought up. But, in experiments where children of different sexes are treated identically, boys and girls tend to behave differently. Here's how the differences begin to show themselves from an early age.

● **A few hours old:** Girl babies are more sensitive to touch than boys.

● **2–4 hours old:** Girl babies will maintain eye contact with a silent adult for twice as long as boys, while boys are as interested in objects as they are in people.

● **3 years old:** Ninety-nine per cent of the speech of girls can be understood. Boys take a year longer. Boys want to explore areas and spaces. Girls prefer to talk and listen.

● **Starting school:** Girls take an average 92.5 seconds to say goodbye to mum at the school gate. Boys rush off after 36 seconds, eager to play.
  Boys prefer toys that do something (e.g. cars). They build tall blocks with building bricks. Girls, in contrast, build long, low buildings.
  Girls like methodical, turn-taking games, like hopscotch. Boys prefer aggressive games with plenty of conflict, like tag.
  In the early days, education favours girls. Boys learn visually and a lot of learning in primary schools involves listening to the teacher. Girls are better readers. Four out of five dyslexics are boys.

● **In the teens:** Lessons now rely more on the visual and boys overtake girls, especially in subjects like science which require experimentation and seeing how things work. At this stage in their lives, hormones tend to make boys more aggressive than girls. Men are five times more likely to commit murder than women and 20 times more likely to commit robbery.

● **Later in life:** Hormone levels in males begin to decline and they gradually become less aggressive. By retirement age, the two sexes are more alike than ever before in their lives.

UNIT 8 LESSON 1

4

Using the information in the text, decide if the following statements are correct. If they are not, correct them.

1 Girls are more mobile than boys at an early age.
2 Girls learn to speak earlier than boys.
3 Boys are closer to their mothers.
4 Boys are naturally aggressive.
5 Girls learn to read more slowly than boys.
6 Men become less aggressive as they grow older.

5

In groups discuss whether you agree with what the article says. Did any information in the text surprise you?

6

Look at the quiz. Tick the answers for yourself, and then compare your answers with a partner. How much do you think it really tells you about yourself or your partner?

1 You hear an indistinct meow. How accurately can you say where the cat is without looking round?
 a You think you could point to it.
 b You could point straight at it.
 c You don't know where it is.

2 How well can you remember a song you've just heard?
 a Easily, and you can sing a bit of it.
 b Only if it's simple and has a very strong tune.
 c With difficulty.

3 How instantly can you recognise the voice of a casual acquaintance on the phone?
 a Quite easily.
 b At least half the time.
 c Less than half the time.

4 If you were out with a group of friends, could you tell that two of them had recently had an argument and there was tension between them?
 a Nearly always.
 b Half the time.
 c Seldom.

5 At a party you meet five strangers. Hearing their names the next day, could you remember their faces?
 a Most of them.
 b A few.
 c Hardly any of them.

6 In your school days how did you find spelling and essays?
 a Both quite easy.
 b One was easy.
 c Neither was easy.

7 You see a parking space, but it's a tight squeeze. What do you do?
 a Look for another.
 b Reverse in very carefully.
 c Reverse in without thinking about it.

8 After three days living in a strange village, would you know where north was?
 a Unlikely.
 b You could work it out.
 c Yes.

9 In a dentist's waiting room with six other people of your own sex, how close could you sit to one of them without feeling distinctly uncomfortable?
 a Less than 15 centimetres.
 b 15 centimetres to 0.5 metres.
 c Over 0.5 metres.

10 Talking to a friend in her quiet house, there's a tap dripping in the background.
 a You notice the sound immediately and try to ignore it.
 b If you notice, you mention it.
 c It doesn't bother you.

HOW TO SCORE

Women
a = 15 points; b = 5 points; take off 5 points for every c that you ticked.

Men
a = 10 points; b = 5 points; take off 5 points for every c that you ticked.

HOW DID YOU DO?

Most men score 0–60. Most women score 50–100. The area between 50 and 60 indicates compatibility between the sexes. Men who score below 0 and women scoring over 100 have very different brains. Men scoring above 60 may have brains that are more characteristic of women, and women scoring below 50 may have brains which are more characteristic of men.

However, these are only average differences between the sexes.

Do the results agree with your own assessment?

Homework

Write a paragraph summarising the differences between the sexes described in this lesson. Then say whether you think these differences are true or not. Give your reasons.

Language Summary

Comparative forms of adjectives
 Girl babies are **more sensitive** to touch **than** boys.
 Girls are **closer** to their mothers **than** boys.

Comparisons: equality and inequality
 Boys are **as interested** in objects **as** they are in people.
 Men become **less aggressive than** women as they become older.

Comparisons: adverbs
 Girls learn to read **more quickly than** boys.
 Boys take a year **longer than** girls.

see practice page 87

Unit 8 All in the mind

Lesson 2 *It's the way you use it*

Language focus:	Conditional sentences in reported speech
Skills focus:	Reading for main ideas Listening: problem solving

1

Solve the following problem in pairs: Make the shape of a wineglass with four matches and put a coin inside the wineglass as shown in the diagram. You have to get the coin out of the wineglass. You can move two of the matches but you cannot touch the coin or push it with one of the matches. The shape of the wineglass must stay the same.

Do you know any other similar puzzles?

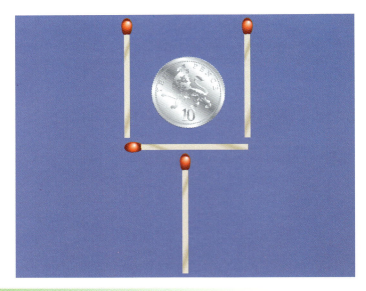

2

Look at the following problem. In groups, decide what possible actions the girl can take. Make a list of your ideas, your reasons and how you reached your decisions.

Many years ago, when a person who owed money could be thrown into jail, a merchant in London had the misfortune to owe a huge sum to a money-lender. The money-lender, who was old and ugly, wanted to marry the merchant's beautiful young daughter. He proposed a deal. He said he would cancel the merchant's debt if he could marry the girl instead.

Both the merchant and his daughter were horrified at the proposal. So the cunning money-lender suggested that they let Providence decide the matter. He told them that he would put a black pebble and a white pebble into an empty money-bag and then the girl would have to pick out one of the pebbles. If she chose the black pebble she would become his wife and her father's debt would be cancelled. If she chose the white pebble she would stay with her father and the debt would still be cancelled. But if she refused to pick out a pebble her father would be thrown into jail and she would starve.

Reluctantly the merchant agreed. They were standing on a pebble-strewn path in the merchant's garden as they talked and the money-lender stooped down to pick up the two pebbles. As he picked up the pebbles the girl, sharp-eyed with fright, noticed that he picked up two black pebbles and put them into the money-bag. He then asked the girl to pick out the pebble that was to decide her fate and that of her father.

Imagine that you are standing on that path in the merchant's garden. What would you have done if you had been the unfortunate girl? If you had had to advise her, what would you have advised her to do?

UNIT 8 LESSON 2

3

 Listen to the solution and compare it with your ideas. What do you think of the solution?

4

Read the following text. What are the two ways of thinking that can help you to solve problems?

> What type of thinking would you use to solve the problem of the merchant's daughter? You may believe that careful logical analysis must solve the problem if there is a solution. This type of thinking is straightforward vertical thinking. The other type of thinking is lateral thinking.
>
> Vertical thinkers are not usually of much help to a girl in this situation. There are only three possibilities in the way they would analyse it.
> 1 The girl should refuse to take a pebble.
> 2 The girl should show that there are two black pebbles in the bag and expose the money-lender as a cheat.
> 3 The girl should take a black pebble and sacrifice herself in order to save her father from prison.
>
> None of the suggestions is very helpful, for if the girl does not take a pebble her father goes to prison, and if she does take a pebble, then she has to marry the money-lender.
>
> The story shows the difference between vertical thinking and lateral thinking. Vertical thinkers are concerned with the fact that the girl has to take a pebble. Lateral thinkers become concerned with the pebble that is left behind. Vertical thinkers take the most reasonable view of a situation and then proceed logically and carefully to work it out. Lateral thinkers tend to explore all the different ways of looking at something, rather than accepting the most promising and proceeding from that.

Look at the following words and decide whether they refer to vertical or lateral thinking. Then complete the two definitions.

| analytical   creative   exploratory   imaginative |
| logical   reasoned   sensible |

1 _____ thinking is _____
2 _____ thinking is _____

Write your own lateral thinking puzzle or write one you know.

5

Decide which type of thinking you used in your group to solve the problem.

6

Here are three more problems. Read the first one. In groups try to solve it, and then listen to the solution. Now try to solve the other two problems using lateral thinking.

1 A man is driving with his son, and they have an accident. In the hospital, the doctor takes one look at the boy and says 'That's my son!' How can this be?

2 A factory employee dreamed one night that his boss would be killed in a train crash the following day. He rang his boss, and told her not to catch the train. His boss caught a different train, and avoided the crash. When she arrived at work she thanked the man, then sacked him. Why?

3 A man lives on the 18th floor of a block of flats. Every morning when he goes to work he takes the lift to the ground floor. If the weather is fine, when he comes home in the evening he takes the lift to the 7th floor and walks the rest of the way up the stairs. If it is raining he takes the lift all the way to the 18th floor. Why?

7

Now listen to two other people discussing the answers to problems 2 and 3, and see if you were right. Did you come up with any different solutions?

Language Summary

Conditional sentences in reported speech
First conditional
  The girl said that **if** he **looked** into the bag he **would be able to** tell which pebble she had taken.

Second conditional
  The writer said that **if** you **used** lateral thinking, you **would find** a solution.

Third conditional
  The writer said that **if** the money-lender **had been** honest she **would have had** only a fifty-fifty chance.

see practice page 88

Unit 8 All in the mind

Lesson 3 *It's on the tip of my tongue*

Language focus: Verbs with infinitive and *-ing* form

Skills focus: Reading: to complete a text and for main ideas
Speaking: exchanging information

1

How good is your memory? Listen to people talking about things they need to do. Try to remember what they say, but don't take any notes.

2

Remembering names is often difficult. Do you have any methods for remembering them? Read the text below on how to remember names and in pairs fill in the missing words from the box.

| at | by | commonest | crawling | feature |
| for | for | in | might | name | should | with |

How to remember names …

An inability to remember names is the (1) _____ complaint that people make about their memories. But there is a simple strategy for improving memory: (2) _____ picturing the name associated with an outstanding (3) _____ of the face.

(4) _____ example, my dentist has fair hair, an angular face and the (5) _____ Bryant. You (6) _____ represent this as bright and then imagine ants, like fireflies (7) _____ out of her hair. Studies show that use of this technique can improve people's memory (8) _____ names by 80 per cent, according to Dr Michael Gruneberg. It (9) _____ however, be used (10) _____ discretion. He said: (11) _____ my experience it is quite impossible to create a useful image and hold a sensible conversation (12) _____ the same time.'

3

Work in pairs. Try to write down the list of things you heard at the beginning of the lesson. Compare your results with another pair. Then listen to the tape again, and see how many you remembered correctly.

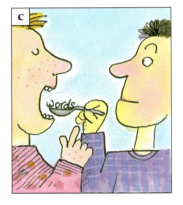 

4

Look at these pictures, which each show an idiom. Match each picture to the correct definition.

1 on the tip of your tongue
2 putting words into someone's mouth
3 a mine of information
4 a memory like a sieve

Now match the idiom to the correct definition below.

a being unable to remember things for long
b reporting what someone has said with your own bias
c almost able to remember something but not quite
d having a lot of facts in your memory

Compare your answers in pairs. This technique of visualising words is similar to the one described in the text in Activity 2. How useful do you think it is?

5

How important do you think a good memory is? In pairs, write a list of as many situations or jobs as you can in which a good memory is vital.

UNIT 8 LESSON 3

6

Read the text quickly to see how many of your ideas are mentioned. Add any other ideas in the text to your list.

A Russian named Shereshevskii could recall perfectly 70 words or numbers presented to him only once. He would then reproduce them in reverse order. Most remarkably, he could still produce the list 15 years later.

This may be of little practical value, but it is a stark contrast to the sieve-like memories most of us have. Yet research shows that we are all capable of training and improving our memories.

Developing techniques for improving memory is now the fastest growing area of psychological research in Europe and America. Most techniques work by providing some kind of association between the thing you want to remember and a visual picture that is easy to recall.

People in many occupations require particular memory skills where these techniques can be useful. Teachers, salespeople and diplomats need a good memory for names, poker players for cards, and supermarket managers for lists of prices.

The difference between someone who has a good memory and someone who hasn't is not one of capacity, but of order. Most people use their memories like a cardboard box: they just throw information in and hope that they can find it later.

The secret of a good memory is mental filing. That takes effort. Remembering is a learned skill that involves hard work.

For public speakers, a good memory is often critical. The American author, Mark Twain, devised a system for remembering his speeches. A haystack with a wiggly line under it to represent a rattlesnake would remind him to begin talking about ranch life in the West. He would draw pictures for all the sections of his speech, all strung out in a row. Then he would look at them and destroy them. When he spoke, the row of images was sharp in his mind. He never needed to consult notes. His system was so good that he could recall speeches given twenty-five years earlier.

Twain was employing a feature of memory that has since been confirmed by research – that images are more memorable than words. The capacity of memory for pictures may be almost unlimited. In experiments, people shown up to 10,000 pictures could later select those they had seen from among unfamiliar ones with remarkable accuracy.

7

Which of the following things does the article say are important in developing a good memory?

confidence   learning by heart
logical organisation   repetition
visualisation   writing notes

8

In pairs, choose one of the idioms below and think of a technique to help you remember it. Compare your ideas with the others in the class, and discuss the best ideas. Use a dictionary to check meaning if you need to.

a blind date   a bookworm
a grey area   jumping to conclusions
a one-track mind   a wet blanket

Homework

Using the notes you made from the text, write a summary of the main ideas in the article under the heading 'The secret of a good memory'.

Language Summary

Verbs with infinitive and -ing form
  I am **unable to remember** names.
  I **enjoy** (doing) memory tests.
  I **remembered to buy/buying** the bread.

see practice page 89

Unit 9 Confidence

Lesson 1 *Recognising yourself*

Language focus: Reflexive verbs
Verb and preposition combinations

Skills focus: Listening for main ideas and detail
Reading and answering a quiz

1

Look at the picture of Cinderella. What kind of person is she in the popular fairy story? What kind of person is the Cinderella in this cartoon?

2

Read this text. Where do you think it comes from? Who do you think wrote it? Do you think this is true?

> *You will always be what you believe you are. The way out of the maze of failure is to believe in yourself. Know that you can be whatever you want to be. When you are aware of yourself and your unlimited potential, you can look at the world and know there are no limitations, only different ways of accomplishing the same thing.*

In pairs, think about these influences on people's lives. Choose the five that you think are the most important. Then number them in order with 1 being the most important.

> appearance   confidence   education
> influence of relatives   male or female   money
> parents   position in the family   self-image
> teachers   upbringing

Compare your list with others in the class, and discuss your reasons for your choices.

3

Listen to a counsellor talking about self-confidence and potential and answer the following questions.

1 What influences on people's confidence does she mention?
2 Which does she feel is the most important and why?
3 What can people who are not confident do to help themselves?

4

In pairs, try to define self-confidence, and complete the sentences.

Self-confidence is _____.

Self-confidence is not _____.

Compare your ideas with the rest of the class, then listen again to the counsellor.

5

How do you think people show self-confidence? In groups, look at the list and decide which behaviour shows confidence and which shows lack of confidence.

1 speaking in a whisper
2 leaning back in your chair
3 short, quick breathing
4 standing tall and straight
5 hunching your shoulders
6 taking time to answer questions
7 talking quickly
8 leaning forward to listen to people
9 rushing to fill silence in conversation
10 playing with your hair

Can you add any other behaviour to the list which shows either confidence or lack of confidence?

6

Listen to the counsellor talking about ways in which people show confidence, and see if your list is the same as what she says.

7

How confident do you think you are? Do the quiz and find out.

UNIT 9 LESSON 1

QUIZ

1 Half an hour before you are due to meet a friend, she rings you up to say that she's too tired to go out that night. Do you …
a think that this means she's losing interest in you?
b accept it without getting annoyed because you don't want to start an argument?
c get annoyed and tell her that you would rather go out with someone else anyway?
d thank her for ringing, but make it clear you are disappointed and would have appreciated time to plan something else?

2 You feel you deserve a rise at work. How do you bring up the subject with your boss?
a Nervously, apologising for wasting their time, and muttering that you could use a little more money.
b You wouldn't dare ask at all.
c By stating your position clearly and giving logical and clear reasons for wanting more money.
d Aggressively, because you feel that you have been exploited.

3 In a shop, you are given the wrong change. Do you …
a do nothing – it's not worth making a fuss?
b tell the salesperson and do your best to get the money?
c point out the mistake, but apologise as soon as the salesperson denies making a mistake?
d accuse the salesperson of trying to cheat you and threaten to call the police unless you get your money back?

4 You and your friends are planning a holiday, but no one can agree where to go. Do you …
a tell them where you would like to go but add that you don't really mind?
b refuse to go if you don't get your own way because it will be a waste of money and you won't enjoy the holiday?
c keep your opinions secret, as you don't want to argue about it?
d try to persuade everyone to agree with you, but give in if you can't convince them?

5 How would you feel about going to a party alone where the only person you know is the host?
a Nervous: you'd probably stay close to the host the whole evening and leave early.
b A little nervous, but you'd try to chat to people you didn't know.
c Fine: you'd invite a friend to go with you so that you didn't have to talk to strangers.
d Terrified: you'd make up a good excuse and stay at home to watch TV.

To find out your confidence rating, look at the key at the bottom of the page. Work out whether you're mostly red, blue, green or yellow by checking which boxes you've ticked.

MOSTLY REDS
You may seem super confident, but your suspicious and aggressive manner shows that you're actually trying to hide a lack of confidence. Although you make a point of displaying confidence, you probably come across as aggressive, not self-assured. Being confident doesn't mean trampling over anyone who stands in your way. A truly confident person doesn't need to do this.

MOSTLY BLUES
With the confidence to accept the difficult times and get on with what's important to you, you're pretty well balanced. You have some insecurities, but these just show that you're human. You're strong enough to stand your ground, but you never feel the need to put people down in an attempt to make yourself appear superior. All this makes you appear confident and you are very well-liked!

MOSTLY GREENS
You're slightly lacking in confidence, but you do have the potential to develop a better self-image. Sometimes you don't stand up for yourself because you don't want confrontation and you want people to like you, but being weak won't make you more popular. In fact, you'll gain more respect if people see you mean what you say.

MOSTLY YELLOWS
You probably tell yourself you'd rather settle for a quiet life than cause trouble by standing up for yourself. You do this because you don't have a lot of self-confidence. Don't let everybody treat you like a doormat! Tell them what you want and show them that you are a person with real aims and opinions. Start taking positive steps to boost your self-confidence now!

8

Now exchange score sheets with a partner. Before you look at your partner's score sheet, try to decide what you think the quiz will tell you about your partner.

Homework

Write another situation for the confidence quiz with suitable answers for the red, blue, green and yellow personality types.

Language Summary

Reflexive verbs
 A confident person will always **hold themselves** upright.

Verb and preposition combinations
 Believe in yourself.
 Be **aware of** yourself.

see practice page 90

Unit 9 Confidence

Lesson 2 *Thinking positively*

Language focus: Modal verbs: *can/be able to*
Modal verbs: *need/don't need/needn't*

Skills focus: Listening for specific information
Reading for main ideas and details

1

Look at the photograph. What is this man doing? Which of the following words would you use to describe him?

anxious   brave   courageous   crazy   daring
fearless   foolish   reckless   strong   timid

2

Listen to John, the man in the photograph, talking about himself and answer these questions.

1 How did John lose his sight?
2 Who helped him to overcome his fears?
3 How did positive thinking help John?
4 Were you surprised to learn that John is blind?
5 Do you think John is exceptional or could anyone in his situation have done what he did?

UNIT 9 LESSON 2

3

Read this text about positive thinking.

Choose the sentence below which best sums up the ideas of the text.

1 People fail because they deserve to fail, people succeed because they deserve to succeed.
2 There is no way you can help someone who is determined to fail, so you might as well not try.
3 We often fail because we think badly of ourselves, but if we think positively about ourselves, we can succeed.
4 You can get what you want in life if you are more aggressive.

4

In groups discuss whether or not you agree with the ideas of the text. Do you think that positive thinking is all you need to improve your life? Do you think that negative thinking is the cause of all our failures?

5

Read the text again and underline the verbs that mean the same as these:

1 to forecast
2 to make better
3 to strengthen or support
4 to succeed in doing something

People make predictions about what will happen to them which are based on their ideas of their own ability or value. For example, Bill, who is a student, says, 'I'll never be able to pass this exam', so instead of studying hard for the exam, he goes out to parties and discos and the prediction comes true when he fails the exam.

Susan, an office worker says, 'I'll never get a pay rise, my boss doesn't value my work, so why should I work hard for nothing?'

She then does the absolute minimum that is required in the job, makes no effort to show initiative and refuses to work any overtime. Not surprisingly, her boss doesn't give her a pay rise at the end of the year.

In countless ways, day after day we live up to our self-image. If that image is negative, we reinforce it. We predict failure, and failure is what we get.

Fortunately, you can predict success as well. To improve your opinion of yourself, behave as if you already have a very positive image of yourself. To improve your chances of having whatever it is in life that you want, imagine yourself having it already. Try writing a letter to the year ahead. Think of next year as a close friend and in your letter tell that friend about the successes you predict for next year, the things you want to achieve, the things you are going to do and all your other goals.

Homework

Write a letter to the year ahead as suggested in the reading text. Outline the successes you predict and the goals you intend to achieve in the year ahead and remember to use positive language!

Language Summary

Modal verbs: *can/be able to*
  You **can do** it.
  I'll never **be able to pass** this exam.

Modal verbs: *need/don't need/needn't*
  I **needed** something to help me overcome my fear of heights.
  There's no **need** for you to fail.

see practice page 91

Unit 9 Confidence

Lesson 3 *Expressing yourself*

Language focus: Adverbs of frequency
Adverbs of manner
It's time + past tense (subjunctive)

Skills focus: Reading for main ideas
Writing: dialogues
Listening: completing a table

1

Look at these two pictures. Imagine you were in the same situations. Would you say anything? If so, what would you say?

2

Have you ever been in a similar situation where you wanted to ask someone to do something (or not to do something), but you didn't? Why didn't you say anything? Discuss in pairs.

In pairs, make a list of the advantages and disadvantages of always saying what you think and feel. Compare your ideas with another pair.

58

UNIT 9 LESSON 3

3

Read the following text and answer the question below.

> One of the problems with saying what you feel is finding the right words. Embarrassment at stating their feelings in public makes many people store up their anger or irritation inside them, so that when they do finally say something, it all comes out in an angry rush of words. It is far better to state your feelings clearly and calmly at the beginning, before a situation has developed so far that your anger and frustration lead you to say something far more aggressive than you intended – and something which is likely to be far less effective in remedying the situation. For example, if someone near you lights up a cigarette and you are allergic to smoke, it is better to say something immediately like, 'Excuse me, I'm allergic to smoke, so would you please not smoke', than to wait until the fumes are choking you and you find yourself screaming abuse at the smoker, who may have been quite unaware of the discomfort they were causing. Even worse, of course, is to say nothing at all and spend your whole life suffering from other people's unpleasant habits.
>
> The secret is to be polite but firm. Don't be afraid to tell people how you feel and don't suffer in silence if another person's behaviour is making you uncomfortable.

According to the passage, which of the following (a, b, c, d or e) would be the best response to the situation described?

Your soup arrives cold in a restaurant.
a Say nothing and drink the soup.
b Say nothing, but don't drink the soup.
c Call the waiter and shout 'This soup's cold. Bring me another one immediately!'
d Call the waiter and say, 'I'm afraid this soup is cold. Would you bring me another bowl, please?'
e Drink the soup but refuse to pay the bill at the end of the meal.

Which sentence is the most polite?

4

Work in pairs and write five possible responses to the following situations.

1 A shop assistant is rude and unhelpful.
2 A friend tells your classmates an embarrassing secret about you.
3 Your neighbour plays very loud music late at night.
4 Your telephone rings in the middle of the night; it is a wrong number.
5 A very heavy person is standing on your foot on a bus.

Now with your partner choose one of the situations and write a dialogue to act out in class.

5

Listen to someone giving practical advice about ways of overcoming the problems of expressing one's feelings.

What advice does the counsellor give? Fill in the table and then compare your answers in groups.

Do	Don't

In groups discuss which piece of advice you feel is the most useful.

Homework

Write two conversations between the people in either of the two pictures on pp 58, one in which the woman successfully communicates her feelings and one in which she fails.

Language Summary

Adverbs of frequency
   I have **never** been able to say what I really feel.

Adverbs of manner
   He spoke to her **angrily**.

It's time + past tense (subjunctive)
   It's time you **said** something.

see practice page 92

Unit 10 The right thing to do

Lesson 1 *The morning*

Language focus: Time clauses with *before, after, once*
Clauses with *having*
Past continuous for future in the past

Skills focus: Reading for main ideas; predicting
Listening for gist

1

Look at the pictures of Jack and of the town where he lives. In pairs, decide what kind of a person Jack is, what sort of job he has got, and if he is happy. What do you think of his town, would you like to live in a place like this?

2

Read the text about Jack, and decide if the statements are true or false. If you think they are false, try to correct them.

1 Jack always talks to his wife a lot at breakfast.
2 Jack normally goes to work by bus.
3 Jack went to work as usual that day.
4 Jack had taken his overalls to work in a parcel.
5 René is also married.
6 Jack feels guilty about meeting René.

Jack Boden got up as usual at seven o'clock, and his wife set a breakfast of bacon and egg before him. They never said much, and spoke even less on this particular morning because both were solidly locked in their separate thoughts which, unknown to each other, they were at last intending to act on.

Instead of getting a bus to his foundry, Jack boarded one for the city centre. He sought out a public lavatory where he was able to take off his overalls, and emerge with them under his arm. They were wrapped in the brown paper which he had quietly put into his pocket as he called to his wife: 'So long, love. See you this afternoon.'

Now wearing a suit, he walked to the railway station. There he met René. Having worked in the same factory, they had, as many others who were employed there saw, 'fallen for each other'. René wasn't married, so there seemed nothing to stop her going away with him. And Jack's dull toothache of a conscience had, in the six months since knowing her, cured itself at last.

3

What do you imagine Jack's wife is like? Discuss your ideas with a partner, and write down some words to describe the sort of person you think she might be.

UNIT 10 LESSON 1

4

Now read the text, and compare your ideas.

No sooner had Jack left for the foundry than his wife, Edna, woke Enoch. She watched him eat; he looked up, half out of his sleep, and didn't smile back at her.

She kissed him, pushed sixpence into his pocket, and sent him up the street to school, then went upstairs to decide what things to take with her. It wasn't a hard choice, for though they had plenty of possessions, little of it was movable. So it turned out that two suitcases and a handbag held all she wanted.

They'd been married ten years, and for seven at least she'd had enough. The trouble with Jack was that he'd let nothing worry him. He was so trustworthy and easygoing he got on her nerves. He didn't even seem interested in other women, and the worst thing about such a man was that he hardly ever noticed when you were upset. When he did, he accused you of upsetting him.

There were so many things wrong, that now she was about to leave she couldn't bring them to mind, and this irritated her, and made her think that it had been even worse than it was. As a couple they had given up tackling any differences between them by the human method of talking. It was as if the sight of each other struck them dumb. On first meeting, a dozen years ago, they had been unable to say much – which, in their mutual attraction, they had confused with love at first sight. And nowadays they didn't try to talk to each other about the way they felt any more because neither of them thought it would do any good. Having come this far, the only thing left was to act. It wasn't that life was dull exactly, but they had nothing in common. If they had, maybe she could have put up with him.

For a week she'd been trying to write a letter, to be posted from where she was going, but she couldn't get beyond: 'I'm leaving you for good, so stop bothering about me any more. Just look after Enoch, because I've had enough and I'm off.' After re-reading it she put it back and shut her handbag.

Having decided to act after years of thinking about it, she was now uncertain as to what she would do. A sister lived in Hull, so her first plan was to stay there till she found a job and a room. This was something to hang on to, and beyond it she didn't think. She'd just have to act again, and that was that. Once you started there was probably no stopping, she thought, not feeling too good about it now that the time had come.

5

At the end of the text it says that Edna 'was not feeling too good about it now that the time had come'. In pairs discuss what time you think this is. What is she planning to do?

6

In groups, discuss what you think is going to happen next. What will happen to Enoch?

7

Now listen to see what happens, and compare your ideas.

Language Summary

Time clauses with *before, after, once*
  Before leaving the house, he put the letter in his pocket.
  After re-reading the letter, she put it back in her handbag.
  Once Jack had left for the foundry, Edna woke Enoch.

Clauses with *having*
  Having worked in the same factory they had 'fallen for each other'.

Past continuous for future in the past
  They **were intending** to act.

see practice page 93

Homework

Jack and Edna both mention a letter they are planning to write, explaining their actions. Write either Jack's or Edna's letter.

Unit 10 The right thing to do

Lesson 2 *The evening*

Language focus:	Conjunctions: *if* replacements (positive and negative) Conjunctions: *although* and *despite/in spite of*
Skills focus:	Reading and listening for specific information

1

Read the description of Enoch, and decide which of the pictures is him.

'Mam,' Enoch cried, going in by the back door. 'Mam, where's my tea?'

He'd come running down the road with a pocketful of marbles. His head in fact looked like one of the more psychedelic ones, with a pale round face, a lick of brilliant ginger hair down over his forehead, and a streak of red toffee-stain across his mouth.

Gossiping again, he thought scornfully, seeing the kitchen empty. He threw his coat onto a chair. The house seemed quieter than usual, he didn't know why. He went into the kitchen and put the kettle on.

Which words in the text helped you to choose the picture?

2

Enoch is returning to an empty house. In pairs, decide what you would do if you were Enoch. Here are some suggestions below:

1 Cook a meal for yourself.
2 Go round to a neighbour's house.
3 Light the fire.
4 Worry about what had happened to your parents.
5 Stay up late.
6 Call the police.

3

Now read the text to see what Enoch actually did.

The tea wasn't like his mother made it. It was too weak. But it was hot, so he put a lot of sugar in to make up for it, then sat at the table to read a comic.

It was early spring, and as soon as it began to get dark he switched the light on and went to draw the curtains. One half came over easily, but the other only part of the way, leaving a foot-wide gap of dusk. This bothered him for a while, until it got dark, when he decided to ignore it and switch the television on.

He began to wonder where his father was. If his mother had gone to Aunt Jenny's and missed the bus home, maybe his father had had an accident at the foundry and fallen into one of the moulds – from which it was impossible to get out alive, except as a skeleton.

Jam pot, butter dish, knife and crumbs were spread over the kitchen table when he got himself something to eat. Not that it bothered him, that his father might have been killed, because when they had left him for an hour on his own a few months ago he had wondered what he would do if they never came back. Before he'd had time to decide, though, they had opened the door to tell him to be off to bed sharp, otherwise he'd be too tired to get up for school in the morning. So he knew they'd be back sooner than he expected. When Johnny Bootle's father had been killed in a lorry last year he'd envied him, but Johnny Bootle himself hadn't liked it very much.

Whether they came back or not, it was nice being in the house on his own. He was boss of it, could make another pot of tea if he felt like it, and keep the gas fire burning as long as he liked. The telly was flickering but he didn't want to switch it off. He turned to scoop a spoonful of raspberry jam from the pot, and swallowed some more cold tea.

UNIT 10 LESSON 2

He sat in his father's chair by the fire, legs stretched across the rug, but ready to jump at the click of the door, and be back at the table before they could get into the room. His father wouldn't like him being in his chair, unless he were sitting on his knee. All he needed was a cigarette, and though he looked on the sideboard and along the shelf there were none in sight. He had to content himself with trying to whistle in a manly style.

If they didn't come back tonight he wouldn't go to school in the morning. They'd be angry when they found out, but that didn't matter if they were dead. It was eight o'clock, and he wondered where they were. They ought to be back by now and he began to regret that he'd hoped they never would be.

4

Read the following statements and decide if they are true or false. Then read the text again to check. Find a reason from the text to justify your answers.

1 Enoch's parents had left him before.
2 Enoch was able to make himself a meal.
3 Enoch was not afraid to be in the house alone.
4 Enoch tried to behave as the man of the house.
5 Enoch accepted the fact that his parents had left.
6 Enoch found it exciting to be alone.

5

Which adverbs would you choose to describe the way in which Enoch reacts to the situation? Use a dictionary to check any words you are not sure of.

**childishly   foolishly   intelligently   irresponsibly
playfully   practically   resourcefully   sensibly**

Which adjectives do you think best describe the way Enoch feels?

**apprehensive   brave   excited   frightened
grown-up   tearful   terrified**

In pairs, add any more words to these lists that you think are appropriate.

Homework

Imagine you are Enoch. Write your entry in your diary before you go to sleep. Start like this:

Today a very strange thing happened ...

6

Listen and find out how Enoch spent the rest of the night, and what he did. Put the events in the correct order. Number them 1–6.

He moved the sofa nearer the fire ☐
He made faces at himself in the mirror ☐
He turned down the gas fire ☐
He got himself some cheese ☐
He wound the clock ☐
He rolled up the carpet ☐

Listen again and match the reasons below to the actions above.

a to cheer himself up and stop himself feeling frightened.
b because he was hungry.
c to make it last longer.
d to give himself confidence in routine.
e to avoid having to go upstairs to sleep.
f to use as a blanket.

Language Summary

Conjunctions: *if* replacements (positive and negative)
If/As long as/Provided they didn't find out, they wouldn't be angry.
When/As soon as they found out, they'd be angry.
Whether they found out **or not**, they'd be angry.

If you **don't go** to bed, you'**ll** be tired tomorrow.
Unless you **go** to bed, you'**ll** be tired tomorrow.
Go to bed, **otherwise** you'**ll** be tired tomorrow.

Conjunctions: *although* and *despite/in spite of*
Although he had eaten some bread and jam, he was still hungry.
Despite/In spite of (eating) the bread and jam he was still hungry.

see practice page 94

Unit 10 The right thing to do

Lesson 3 *The next day*

Language focus: Present wishes
Past regrets

Skills focus: Reading for specific information
Speaking: roleplaying a conversation

1

Work in pairs. Summarise the story so far.

2

Read the text, which tells you what Enoch did when he woke up the next day. In pairs, decide which of the five sentences below go into the three spaces in the text.

a He went into the kitchen to wash his face.
b He decided to cook himself some breakfast.
c Apart from not wanting to spend the sixpence his mother had given him, he was sorry at having to go to his grandma's because now he wouldn't be able to go to school and tell his mates that he'd been all night in a house on his own.
d He wondered why his eyelids were stuck together, then thought of chopping up a chair to make a blaze, but the grate was blocked by the gas fire.
e He decided to stay in the house to wait for his parents to come home.

He sniffed the cold air, and sensed there was daylight in it, though he couldn't open his eyes. Weaving his hand as far as it would go, he felt that the gas fire had gone out, meaning that the cooking stove wouldn't work. (1) _____

This disappointed him, because it would have been nice to lean over it, warming himself as the bottom of the kettle got blacker and blacker till it boiled at the top.

When his eyes mysteriously opened, old Tinface the clock said it was half past seven. In any case there were no matches left to light anything. (2) _____

He had to be content with a cup of milk, and a spoon of sugar in it, with more bread and cheese. People were walking along the backyards on their way to work. If they've gone for good, he thought, I shall go to my grandma's, and I'll have to change schools because she lives at Netherfield, miles away.

His mother had given him sixpence for sweets the morning before, and he already had tuppence, so he knew that this was enough to get him half fare to Netherfield.

That's all I can do, he thought, wondering whether he ought to put the furniture right in case his parents came in and got mad that it was all over the place, though he hoped they wouldn't care, since they'd left him all night on his own. (3) _____

What does Enoch decide to do at the end?

3

Look at the picture of Enoch's grandmother. What sort of person do you think she is? In pairs, imagine what Enoch will tell his grandmother when he arrives at her house, what she will say in reply, what her reaction will be to Enoch's news and what she will suggest. Write the dialogue and then roleplay the conversation.

4

 Listen to the conversation between Enoch and his grandmother. Is it similar to your dialogue?

5

Decide which of the following words describe her reaction best.

> amusement anger concern fury
> hysteria shock surprise worry

In pairs, discuss your choices and give your reasons. Try to guess what the end of the story might be.

UNIT 10 LESSON 3

6

Now read the last part of the story and answer the questions below.

1 What does Enoch's grandmother say that he should have done when his parents didn't come home?
2 Why didn't Enoch go to a neighbour's house?
3 Why does Enoch follow his grandmother around the house?
4 What are the letters that Enoch's grandmother picks up?

She held his hand back to the bus stop. It seemed years already since he'd last seen his mother and father, and he was growing to like the adventure of it, provided they didn't stay away too long. It was
5 rare going twice across town in one day.

It started to rain, so they stood in a shop doorway to wait for the bus. The bus wasn't so crowded this time and they sat on the bottom deck because his grandma didn't want to climb the stairs.

10 'Did you lock the door behind you?'

'I forgot.'

'Let's hope nobody goes in.'

'There was no light left,' he said. 'nor any gas. I was cold when I woke up.'

15 'I'm sure you were,' she said. 'But you're a big boy now. You should have gone to a neighbour's house. They'd have given you some tea. Mrs Upton would, I'm sure. Or Mrs Mackley.'

'I kept thinking they'd be back any minute.'

20 If it happened again, he would take her advice. He hoped it wouldn't, though; next time he'd sleep in his bed and not be frightened.

They walked down the yard, and in by the back door. The empty house seemed dead, and he didn't
25 like that. He couldn't stay on his own, so he followed his grandmother upstairs and into every room, half expecting her to find them in some secret place he'd never known of.

The beds were made, and wardrobe doors closed.
30 One of the windows was open a few inches, so she slammed it shut and locked it. 'Come on down. There's nothing up here.'

She put a shilling in the gas meter, and set a kettle on the stove. 'Might as well have a cup of tea while
35 I think this one out. A bloody big one it is, as well.'

It was the first time he'd heard her swear, but then, he'd never seen her worried, either. It made him feel better. She went into the front room and he followed her.

40 'They kept the house clean, anyway,' she said, touching the curtains and chair covers.

He agreed, and then saw two letters lying on the mat just inside the front door. He watched her broad back as she bent to pick them up, thinking
45 now that they were both dead for sure.

7

Do you think that this is a good end to the story? Why/why not? How would you have liked it to end?

8

In groups, decide whether Jack and Edna were right to go away. Explain your reasons to the rest of the class. What do you think will be the effect on Enoch of his parents' desertion?

Homework

Have you heard any other stories about children left alone by their parents? Write a short account of one of these stories explaining what happened and why the parents left the child.

Language Summary

Present wishes
  I **wish** my parents **were** here.
  He **wishes** he **had** some cigarettes.
  I **wish** I **could** go to school tomorrow.

Past regrets
  He **wishes** he **hadn't cried** in front of his grandmother.

see practice page 95

Unit 1 Lesson 1

Language Summary

Past simple and past continuous

I **walked** along the front of the school.
Use past simple to talk about single past events.

They **were wrestling** and **rolling** and **screaming** and **shouting**.
Use past continuous to talk about something which was in progress at a past time.

It **was raining** when I **walked** to school.
As I **was getting** ready for school, my brother **asked** me to lend him some money.
Use both when one past action is longer than another or when one is interrupted by the other.

1

Put the verbs in brackets into the most suitable tense, either past simple or past continuous.

1 When Jimmy _entered_ (enter) the playground, the children _were running_ (run) round.
2 The children _____ (wrestle) and _____ (play) noisily when Jimmy _____ (arrive).
3 Jimmy suddenly _____ (feel) very nervous and lonely.
4 A boy _____ (stop) in front of him and _____ (ask) him for his name.
5 Jimmy _____ (tell) the boy his name and the boy _____ (start) to laugh and dance.
6 While Jimmy _____ (talk) to the boys, a teacher _____ (watch) from the school window.
7 While he _____ (watch) the boys, the teacher _____ (wonder) who the new boy was.
8 When he _____ (be) at school, Jimmy always _____ (wear) a school uniform.

2

In this text, underline all the verbs in the past continuous tense. Decide whether this tense has been used correctly in each case and change it if it has not.

I'll never forget my first day at secondary school. I was being so excited that I wasn't being able to sleep the night before. I was getting up early and meeting my friend at the gate so that we could walk to school together. We were looking around, both of us were being a bit lively and daft, and I wasn't seeing the car behind us. I was tripping on the kerb, falling into the road, and the car was hitting me on the back of the leg. I was being in hospital for a month. All this because I wasn't looking where I was going.

Vocabulary

3

Match the beginning of the sentences on the left with the best ending from the list on the right.

1 I was looking forward to
2 I was wondering what
3 I couldn't wait
4 I'm really keen
5 It took quite a time to
6 I wondered whether
7 I was so excited that
8 I felt as though I'd

build up some friends.
the other boys would be like.
joined the real world.
on music and rhythm.
to get away from my old school.
I couldn't sleep the night before.
the teachers would be nice.
being the same as the others.

4

Write the noun equivalents for the adjectives on the left. Mark the stressed syllable on each word as in the example.

1 ex<u>ci</u>ted   ex<u>ci</u>tement
2 <u>an</u>xious   anx<u>ie</u>ty
3 pleased   _____
4 surprised   _____
5 apprehensive   _____
6 sad   _____
7 vulnerable   _____
8 enthusiastic   _____

Unit 1 Lesson 2

Language Summary

Present simple and continuous with present meaning

Everybody **wears** a uniform.
We use present simple for things that happen always or generally.

Everybody **is praising** the sun.
We use present continuous for things happening at or around the moment of speaking.

1

Put the verbs in these passages into either the present simple or the present continuous by crossing out the incorrect form from the pair in brackets.

I (think/am thinking) that social rules are stupid. When I (go/am going) out in the evening, I (tell/am telling) my parents that I am meeting a friend at her house, when in fact we are meeting at the local disco. I never (go/am going) home at the time I (say/am saying) I will. I (take/am taking) a childish pleasure in upsetting my parents. I (don't know/am not knowing) why I (do/am doing) this.

At the moment, I (get on/am getting on) better with my parents than I used to. Perhaps this (means/is meaning) that I (grow up/am growing up). But I still usually (wear/am wearing) clothes they (don't like/aren't liking) and I never (listen/am listening) to their advice. Perhaps they (get used/are getting used) to me and (don't worry/are not worrying) so much these days.

Vocabulary

2

Use a combination of *some/any/every/no* and *where/thing/body* to complete the following sentences.

1 When people do _something_ one way, the rebel does it the opposite way.
2 Rebellious children often hate _____ connected with school.
3 People often think that when _____ is being cheeky, they are being rebellious.
4 Rebels can be found _____ .
5 There is _____ more difficult to live with than a rebellious teenager.
6 Teenagers don't want _____ else making decisions for them
7 There is _____ wrong with teenagers feeling a bit rebellious.
8 Is there _____ that parents can do to help these teenagers?

Pronunciation

3

Put the words below into rhyming pairs.

1 tough   a horse
2 course   b two
3 suede   c cuff
4 wear   d made
5 true   e taught
6 learn   f lane
7 rain   g trees
8 thought   h cart
9 please   i burn
10 heart   j fair

Unit 1 Lesson 3

Language Summary 1

Will for predictions

I think it **will** always happen.
Why will they always contradict everything you say?

We use **will** + infinitive to make predictions about what we think will happen in the future.

1
Join the two ideas to make predictions about the future using *will/won't*.

1 Teenagers/be able to vote at 16.
   In the future teenagers will be able to vote at 16.

2 Teenagers/be able to 'divorce' their parents.

3 The generation gap/get worse.

4 Different generations/understand each other better.

5 Teenage rebellion/become more of a problem.

6 Teenage fashions/become more extreme.

2
Angela is a teenager who has been to see Mike Moran, the youth worker. Below is a list of the problems they discussed. Mike and Angela made some decisions about how Angela could resolve them. Write predictions about what Angela will do using *will* or *won't*.

1 Angela doesn't talk to her parents about her problems.
   Angela will try to talk to her parents about her problems.

2 Angela's parents treat her like a child.
   Angela will ask ...

3 Angela often goes out at night without telling her parents where she is.

4 Angela never comes home at the time she is supposed to.

5 Angela plays her music very loud.

6 Angela's parents always shout at her.

7 Angela doesn't tidy her room very often.

8 Angela doesn't introduce her friends to her parents.

Language Summary 2

Will for annoying habits

Why **will** they always contradict everything you say?
Parents **will** keep interfering.

We use *will* for emphasis when we talk about people's annoying habits. The use of *keep* is also for emphasis and to show that the habit is repeated.

3
Make these complaints more emphatic by using *will*.

1 My brother keeps borrowing my clothes.
   My brothers will keep borrowing my clothes.

2 My mother nags me about my untidy room.

3 My father always compares me with my older brother.

4 My sister tells all her friends my embarrassing secrets.

5 My teachers keep warning me that I'll fail my exams if I don't study harder.

Vocabulary

4
Fill the gaps in the sentences below with suitable words from the box.

| confidential interfere nag |
| strict surly unreasonable yob |

1 My neighbour's son is a _____ . He's untidy, bad-mannered and badly-behaved.

2 I think it is _____ to expect teenagers to behave like adults if you treat them as children.

3 If teenagers tell you about their problems, that information is _____ – you shouldn't tell anyone else.

4 When I was a teenager, I was very _____ : I wouldn't talk to anyone and I seemed to be in a bad mood all the time.

5 I try not to _____ , but my daughter's room is so untidy that I have to say something!

6 Teenagers get angry if their parents _____ in their choice of friends. They feel they have the right to choose their own friends.

7 If parents are too _____ , then teenagers are likely to rebel against their rules.

Unit 2 Lesson 1

Language Summary 1

Present perfect simple

*People **have turned** to belief in UFOs.*
a The present perfect is used to give news about recent events. Here the specific time is not stated.

*There **have been** many sightings in recent years.*
b It is also used to talk about a stated period continuing until the present.

*I'**ve** never actually **seen** anything like a UFO myself.*
(in my life)
c It can also be used to talk about an unstated period continuing until the present.

1

Decide if the following sentences are like type a, b or c above.

1. I don't know anybody who has seen a UFO. _c_
2. There have been a growing number of UFO sightings this year. ____
3. There has been another UFO sighting in the Cotswolds. ____
4. Nobody has succeeded in capturing a UFO. ____
5. I have never been so frightened. ____
6. Peter has told that UFO story three times since Monday. ____
7. A new book about UFOs has just been published. ____
8. Most UFO sightings have occurred this century. ____

Language Summary 2

Present perfect and past simple

*I **have seen** a UFO.*
We can use the present perfect when we know something happened recently, but we don't know when.

*When I was 17 I **saw** a UFO.*
We use the past simple when we know when.

2

Choose the correct form of the verb from the alternatives in brackets.

There (has been/was) another sighting of a UFO over the Cotswolds. It (has happened/happened) last night when Mr Peter Smith (has been/was) walking near his home in Bourton. Mr Smith, who (has lived/lived) in Bourton all his life, (has never seen/never saw) a UFO before and admits that he (has always been/was always) sceptical about them until now. Mr Smith (has left/left) his home at 8.00 o'clock last night with his dog, Rover. It (has been/was) when Rover (has begun/began) barking that Mr Smith (has looked/looked) up and (has seen/saw) a large metallic object in the sky. 'I (have been/was) terrified,' he (has said/said). I (have thrown/threw) myself on the ground and (have covered/covered) my eyes with my hands. When I (have looked/looked) again, it had gone.' Several other people (have reported/reported) seeing bright lights and hearing strange noises in the Bourton area in the last few days. As yet, no one (has given/gave) an explanation for the events.

Language Summary 3

The gerund as subject

***Explaining** why they are sometimes seen by several people at once is hard.*
***It is hard to explain** why they are sometimes seen by several people at once.*

Compare the two sentences above which have the same meaning. Which grammatical structure has changed? What else has changed?

3

Rewrite each of these sentences in the alternative form so that the meaning is not changed.

1. It has never been easy to prove that UFOs exist.
   Proving that UFOs exist has never been easy.
2. Accepting that some people have seen UFOs may be difficult for you.
   _____
3. Assuming that all UFOs come from outer space is ridiculous.
   _____
4. It is interesting to speculate about what life on other planets might be like.
   _____
5. It is unkind to laugh at people who really believe they have seen something.
   _____
6. Checking the authenticity of photographs is not hard.
   _____
7. Describing exactly what you have seen can be impossible.
   _____
8. It is difficult to believe in all the UFO sightings.
   _____

Unit 2 Lesson 2

Language Summary 1

Direct questions
How old were you when you saw the ghosts?
Did you get a good view of them?

1
In this interview with Harry Martindale, complete the questions using the words in brackets.

Reporter: *How old were you when you saw the ghosts?*
 (old/see/ghosts)

Harry: I was eighteen.

Reporter: _____ (do/cellar)

Harry: I was installing central heating.

Reporter: _____ (do/see/ghosts)

Harry: I fell off the ladder and then kept still.

Reporter: _____ (many/them)

Harry: Between twelve and twenty.

Reporter: _____ (look)

Harry: They looked dirty and scruffy.

Reporter: _____ (wear)

Harry: Handmade green cloth clothes.

Reporter: _____ (tall)

Harry: Only about five feet tall.

Reporter: _____ (horse)

Harry: It was a great big cart-horse.

Reporter: _____ (noise)

Harry: Only a sort of murmuring.

Reporter: _____ (do/after)

Harry: I ran up the stairs out of the cellar.

Language Summary 2

Indirect questions
Compare these two pairs of questions:
How old was he when he saw the ghost?
Did he say how old he was when he saw the ghost?
Did you get a good view of them?
Did you ask him if he got a good view of them?

2
Using the information in exercise 1, complete the gaps in the questions below in which the reporter is being asked about the interview with Harry.

1 Did you ask him how *old he was when he saw* the ghosts?
2 Did you ask him what _____ cellar?
3 What did he say he _____ ghosts?
4 Did you ask him how many _____ ?
5 Did he say what _____ ?
6 Did he tell you _____ ?
7 Did you ask him how _____ ?
8 And did he say _____ like?
9 Did he mention whether _____ noise?
10 What did he say _____ gone?

Language Summary 3

Negative words used for emphasis
*I was in **no** fit state to count them.*
***Not one** of them looked in my direction.*
*The horses were **nothing** like the ones they use nowadays on TV.*

3
Put either *no*, *not one* or *nothing* in each of the gaps in these sentences.

1 The men were *nothing* like the Roman soldiers of Hollywood movies.
2 _____ of them was visible below the knee.
3 _____ of the ghosts has ever been photographed.
4 There is _____ evidence whatsoever to support his story.
5 _____ of them spoke a single word.
6 There was _____ unusual about their helmets.
7 There was _____ reason to suppose Harry was lying.

Unit 2 Lesson 3

Language Summary 1

Past passive

We form the past passive with was/were + past participle.

*The tomb **was discovered** by Lord Carnavon and Howard Carter.*
1 The passive is used when the action is more important than the agent.

*A curse **was written** in hieroglyphics.*
2 It is also used when we do not know (or don't want to say) who the agent is.

*The lines **were made** by placing stones in the soil.*
3 It can also be used when we are describing a process.
Note: In types 2 and 3 the agent is usually omitted.

1

Look at each of these active sentences. Change them into the passive and decide whether to use an agent or not. In each case, which sounds better – the active or the passive – or does it make no difference?

1 Carnavon and Carter discovered Tutankhamun's tomb in 1922.
   Tutankhamun's tomb was discovered by Carnavon and Carter in 1922

2 They opened the innermost part of the tomb in February 1923.
   _____

3 Twenty people witnessed the opening of the tomb.
   _____

4 The story inspired a series of Hollywood films.
   _____

5 Somebody made the Nazca lines between 400 BC and 900 AD.
   _____

6 They took out the stones very precisely.
   _____

7 They made thousands of parallel and converging straight lines.
   _____

8 Somebody made lines in the shape of animals.
   _____

Language Summary 2

Modal verbs: deductions and speculations in the past

*They **must have taken** a long time to make.*
It is certain.

*They **could have been** runways for gods to land.*
*They **may have been** launch pads for balloons.*
*They **might have been** pathways to temples.*
It is possible.

*They **can't have served** any practical purpose.*
It is impossible.

2

Read the text on page 16 again and answer these questions about Tutankhamun using the forms above. Give your real opinions.

1 Do you think Tutankhamun was an important man?
   He must have been because he had a lot of treasure.

2 Do you think Carnavon and Carter were frightened by the curse?
   They _____ have been because _____

3 Do you think Carnavon died as a result of the curse?
   He _____ have done because _____

4 Do you think the flickering lights were linked to Carnavon's death?
   _____

5 Do you think the priests left poison in the tombs?
   _____

6 Do you think the curse led to Ezzaddin Taha's death?
   _____

Vocabulary

3

Put one of the words from the box in each of the gaps in the sentences below.

| whoever | whatever | however |
| whichever | wherever | whenever |

1 Death will destroy ___*whoever*___ disturbs the Pharaoh's peace.

2 _____ he did, Carter couldn't forget Tutankhamun.

3 _____ you go, you can't escape the curse.

4 _____ one of the party died, the story of the curse was revived.

5 _____ discovered the Nazca lines must have been in a plane.

6 In _____ direction you walk, you come to more lines.

7 Straightness was important to _____ designed the lines.

8 _____ much research is done, nobody can explain the lines.

Unit 3 Lesson 1

Language Summary 1

Order of adjectives

*He was wearing a **new navy-blue** overcoat.*
The most objective adjective is placed closest to the noun.

*She had a **round pink** face and very **gentle blue** eyes.*
The most subjective adjective is placed closest to the verb.

The order of adjectives before the noun is usually:
1 opinion **2** size **3** age **4** shape **5** colour **6** material **7** type.

1
Put the adjectives in brackets into the correct order before the noun.

1 It's a (medium-sized, three-star, fashionable) hotel.
   It's a fashionable, medium-sized, three-star hotel.

2 He carried an (blue, old, leather) suitcase.

3 He arrived in the (cathedral, fine, old) city.

4 He was wearing a (two-piece, new, brown, smart) suit.

5 He saw a (neglected, old, town, white) house.

6 It had a (hand-written, scruffy, yellow) notice in the window.

7 He sat on an (ancient, uncomfortable, grey) sofa.

8 He would have preferred a (modern, large, brightly-lit) pub.

Language Summary 2

Subclauses without verbs

***Situated near the Royal Crescent**, it offers comfortable, quiet accommodation.*
This type of sentence is common in advertising where economy of space is very important. The clause has no verb. The subject is after the comma.

2
Rewrite each of these pairs of sentences so that there is one new sentence beginning with a verbless subclause.

1 The hotel is close to the city centre. It has parking for 156 cars.
   Close to the city centre, the hotel has parking for 156 cars.

2 The hotel is just 10 minutes walk from the station. It stands amongst landscaped grounds.

3 The Bell and Dragon is about half a mile from the centre. It is a very cheap place to stay.

4 The restaurant is opposite the station. It serves a range of cheap meals.

5 The guest house is next to the motorway. It is the best value in town.

6 The pub is not far from the shopping centre. It offers excellent quick lunches.

Pronunciation

3
Put each of the words in the box into the correct column according to its word stress pattern.

| splendid   obvious   amazing   pleasant |
| decent   comfortable   overcoat   facility   atmosphere |
| crescent   convenient   location |

▫■▫▫	■▫	▫■▫	▫■▫▫
successful	handsome	adjective	identical

Unit 3 Lesson 2

Language Summary 1

Question tags 1

*It is Mr Perkins, **isn't it?***
Positive statements have a negative tag and vice versa.

*They weren't famous in any way, **were they?***
The auxiliary verb is repeated in the tag and the subject and verb are inverted.

1

Add a question tag to each of these statements.

1 You'd like some supper, _wouldn't you_ ?
2 They were tall and handsome, _____ ?
3 You won't forget to sign the book, _____ ?
4 I've heard those names before, _____ ?
5 You haven't met Mr Mulholland, _____ ?
6 You will have a cup of tea, _____ ?
7 This entry is two years old, _____ ?
8 You can afford five and sixpence, _____ ?
9 Mr Temple wasn't from Bristol, _____ ?

Language Summary 2

Question tags 2

*How time flies, **doesn't it?***
When there is no auxiliary verb in the statement, use a form of *do* in the tag.

2

Add a question tag to each of these statements, adding a form of *do*.

1 You don't know Mr Mulholland, _do you_ ?
2 Mr Mulholland came from Bristol, _____ ?
3 This room gets the morning sun, _____ ?
4 She seemed very kind, _____ ?
5 You have sugar in your tea, _____ ?
6 These names seem to be connected, _____ ?
7 You don't like eggs for breakfast, _____ ?
8 Billy finds it extraordinary, _____ ?

Language Summary 3

Intensifiers

*I'm **so** glad you appeared.*
Use *so* with adjectives and adverbs.

***Such** charming boys.*
Use *such* with adjective and noun groups.

*I **do** apologise.*
Use *do* to emphasise verbs.

3

Put either *so*, *such* or a form of *do* into each of the gaps.

1 I'm ___so___ grateful to you.
2 I _____ hope you'll like the room.
3 It's _____ a nice room.
4 I was getting _____ worried.
5 I'm _____ tired, I'll go straight to bed.
6 Please, _____ remember to sign the book.
7 It was _____ a lovely little dog.
8 The names in the book seemed _____ familiar.
9 They _____ sound like names I've heard before.
10 You _____ say you took sugar in your tea, didn't you?

Vocabulary

4

Match each of the words on the left with a word from the list on the right which has an opposite meaning.

1 charming   a host
2 famous   b mean
3 generous   c ugly
4 handsome   d uncertain
5 positive   e rude
6 guest   f unknown

(charming — rude; guest — host)

Unit 3 Lesson 3

Language Summary 1

Short answers for agreement

I'm looking for somewhere to stay.
So am I.
When agreeing with a positive statement, we use *so* + auxiliary (inverted).

I don't want to stay in a hotel.
Neither do I.
When agreeing with a negative statement, we use *neither* + auxiliary (inverted).

1
Write a short response using *so* or *neither* to agree with each of these statements.

1 I saw them in the newspaper. _So did I._
2 Billy takes sugar in tea. _____
3 He is very tired. _____
4 He must go to bed early this evening. _____
5 I've signed the book. _____
6 Billy wasn't very comfortable on the train. _____
7 He couldn't believe the parrot wasn't alive. _____
8 I don't like the taste of this tea. _____

Language Summary 2

Adverbials: modifications of degree

*I suppose he left **fairly** recently.*
There are many adverbials which can be used to modify degree.

2
Look at the underlined word in each of these sentences and decide whether replacing them with the words a–d would make them stronger, weaker or leave them the same.

1 I suppose he left <u>fairly</u> recently.
   a very   _stronger_
   b quite   _the same_
   c really   _stronger_
   d relatively   _the same_

2 I was <u>completely</u> fooled.
   a wholly _____
   b somewhat _____
   c absolutely _____
   d utterly _____

3 It's <u>awfully</u> difficult.
   a terribly _____
   b quite _____
   c pretty _____
   d extremely _____

4 I'm <u>almost</u> positive.
   a relatively _____
   b absolutely _____
   c fairly _____
   d quite _____

5 Mr Temple was <u>a little</u> older.
   a a bit _____
   b a trifle _____
   c much _____
   d slightly _____

Pronunciation

3
Divide the words in the box into six groups according to the main vowel sound.

~~wait~~	way	~~lease~~	sight	~~pick~~	seem	~~that~~
bit	sip	~~stare~~	tea	hand	hate	skin	where
as	care	taste	pat	smile	seat	age	teeth
quite	while	fill	hair	chair	feel	sit

/eɪ/	/æ/	/ɪ/	/iː/	/eə/	/aɪ/
wait	that	pick	lease	stare	sight

Unit 4 Lesson 1

Language Summary 1

Past simple and past perfect

*Danko **had volunteered** to lead them out of the forest ... but the journey **seemed** hard and endless.*

The events in this sentence occurred in this order:
1 Danko volunteered to lead them out of the forest
2 the journey seemed hard and endless.

The past perfect is used for the event that happened first, the past simple for the event that happened second.

1

Put the verbs in brackets into the correct tense. Use the past perfect or past simple.

1 Danko's people ___lived___ (live) in a dark forest because invaders ___had faced___ (force) them to leave their valley.
2 After Danko and his friends _____ (leave) the dark forest, they _____ (go) on a long journey.
3 Everyone _____ (be) so busy celebrating that they _____ (fail) to notice that Danko _____ (die).
4 Thizi _____ (give) Loki his freedom, after Loki _____ (drop) the nut at his feet.
5 The gods _____ (not be) able to become young again until they _____ (eat) the golden apples.
6 Once Loki _____ (transform) himself into a large bird, he _____ (be) able to rescue Idun.
7 Koon-se's father _____ (be) furious because she _____ (fall) in love with Chang.
8 Chang _____ (try) to rescue Koon-se when he _____ (realise) her father _____ (arrange) for her to marry someone else.

2

Using the information from two of the stories in this lesson, complete the following sentences, using either a past simple or past perfect form of the verb.

1 The Gods asked Loki to help because (start/grow/old)

   The Gods asked Loki to help because they'd started to grow old.

2 Loki could fly because he (transform/large bird) _____

3 Thizi captured Loki and (demand/give/golden apples) _____

4 Everything was restored to normal when Loki (return/golden apples) _____

5 Koon-se's father kept her indoors because (love/poor shepherd) _____

6 Koon-se and Chang were able to fly away because (they/change/bluebirds) _____

Language Summary 2

Narrative time markers

Once upon a time *a very rich, important official had a beautiful daughter called Koon-se.*

We use words like *once, at first, finally, then, next*, etc. as time markers in a narrative to show the sequence of events.

3

Put one of the words or phrases from the box into each of the spaces in the passage.

| then   once upon a time   finally   at first |
| once   when   in the end   at the last moment |
| no sooner   as a result |

Once upon a time, there was a very rich, important official who had a beautiful daughter called Koon-se. She fell in love with a poor shepherd called Chang and _____ her father found out, he was furious. _____, he kept his daughter indoors and _____ arranged for her to marry a rich neighbour. _____ had Chang realised than he tried to rescue her by disguising himself as a wedding guest and entering the house. _____ reunited, the two young lovers tried to escape towards the river where a boat was waiting for them. _____, not knowing what else to do, Koon-se prayed to the goddess Kwan-yin, who took pity on the pair and changed them into bluebirds and _____ they were able to escape and be free together.

Unit 4 Lesson 2

Language Summary 1

Used to and past simple

Robin Hood used to rob the rich to give to the poor.
This sentence describes a habit in the past.

Robin shot an arrow into the forest and asked to be buried where it fell.
This sentence describes a single past event.

1
Complete these sentences with the correct form of the verb in brackets. If *used to* is possible, use that form. If it is not, use the past or present simple.

1 Robin Hood ___*lived*___ (live) all his life in Sherwood Forest.
2 He _____ (surprise) people coming through the forest.
3 The Sheriff of Nottingham _____ (search) for Robin in the forest.
4 Before Robin _____ (die), he _____ (shoot) an arrow into the forest.
5 Robin _____ (ask) to be buried where the arrow _____ (land).
6 The exhibition _____ (recreate) the atmosphere of how life _____ (be) at the time of Robin Hood.

Language Summary 2

Used to and would

The most interesting part was seeing how people used to live.
We use *used to* for states in the past and situations which are no longer true.

What they used to/would eat.
We can use either *used to* or *would* for habits/routines in the past.

2
In the text below decide when only *used to* is possible and when both *used to* and *would* are possible.

In the times of Robin Hood, there (used to/would) be many tradespeople in Nottingham and often women (used to/would) work with their husbands and fathers. Blacksmiths (used to/would) work with techniques which are very similar to those of today. In the 'Tales of Robin Hood' exhibition we can get a real idea of what life (used to/would) be like in medieval England. Sherwood Forest (used to/would) be of great importance to the King as a place to hunt, and because it (used to/would) provide him with considerable income. Sherwood Forest, although not as large as it (used to/would) be, still exists near Nottingham and you can visit the area where Robin Hood (used to/would) ambush travellers. The story of Robin Hood (used to/would) be a legend known only in England, but since the release of various films, it has become famous all over the world.

Vocabulary

3
Complete the sentences by choosing the appropriate preposition from the box to form a phrasal verb with *take*.

| over | on | off | up | away |

1 The organisers of the exhibition took ___*over*___ an old supermarket site.
2 The exhibition took _____ as soon as it opened and is a great success.
3 The King took _____ the forest officials to make sure the law was kept.
4 Robin Hood took money _____ from the rich to give to the poor.
5 Robin Hood took _____ stealing for good motives.

4
Match the phrasal verbs in Activity 3 with a synonym from the list below.

a to become popular _____
b to employ _____
c to remove _____
d to take control of _____
e to start _____

Unit 4 Lesson 3

Language Summary

The impersonal passive

The impersonal passive is used to talk about things which may not be true. We are not sure if what we have heard is true or not.

It is believed that she led the French army to free the city of Orléans ...
She is believed to have led the French army to free the city of Orléans ...
People think it is true.

It was said that Joan of Arc was a witch.
Joan of Arc *was said* to have been a witch.
People said that she was a witch.

1

Rewrite the following sentences using the impersonal passive.

1 People believe that Joan of Arc heard voices.
   Joan of Arc _is believed to have heard voices._
   It is _believed that Joan of Arc heard voices._

2 We understand that England occupied most of northern France at that time.
   England _____

3 People believe that voices told Joan how to end the siege.
   It is _____

4 We understand that Joan of Arc led the victorious army.
   Joan of Arc _____

5 People say that the voices told Joan to make sure the Dauphin was crowned.
   It is _____

6 People accused her of being a witch and put her to death.
   She _____

2

Use the following notes to write the sentences in full. Add words and use the passive where appropriate.

1 New exhibition/open/city centre/this week.
   A new exhinition was opened in the city centre this week.

2 Exhibition/about/life/Joan of Arc.
   _____

3 She/understand/burn/to death/Rouen/1431.
   _____

4 Now/think/be/saint.
   _____

5 Exhibition/tell/story/brave/woman.
   _____

6 Include/sound/smell/moving images.
   _____

Vocabulary

3

Complete the sentences using one of the verbs from the box to fill each space.

| brochure   catalogue   directory   leaflet |
| programme   guidebook   prospectus   manual |
| worksheet   phrasebook |

1 We looked through the holiday _brochure_ before deciding to go to Orléans.

2 The museum publishes a _____ giving details of all the exhibits.

3 At the exhibition I picked up a two-page _____, reviewing the main books written about Joan.

4 The museum has computerised displays and a _____ telling you how to operate them.

5 The _____ of the University of Orléans contains a brief history of the town.

6 The number of the museum can be found in the local telephone _____.

7 If you stay in Orléans it is useful to buy a _____ telling you about the whole region.

8 The museum also produces a _____ for groups of visiting schoolchildren.

9 In Orléans we went to the theatre and I kept the _____ as a souvenir.

10 As I don't speak French, my little _____ was invaluable during the holiday.

Unit 5 Lesson 1

Language Summary 1

Reported speech: changes to the verb

Summary of changes:
All present tenses change to past tenses.
All past tenses change to past perfect tense.
The past perfect tense does not change.

Statements
'I **am** still a bit shocked,' Valerie said.
Valerie said that she **was** still a bit shocked.

Wh Questions
'What time **did** the robbery **happen**?' asked the reporter.
The reporter asked what time the robbery **had happened**.

1
Statements
Change sentences 2–5 into direct speech and sentences 6–9 into reported speech.

1. Valerie said that she was still a bit shocked.
   'I'm still a bit shocked,' said Valerie.

2. Valerie said she had been doing her normal work when the man came in.

3. The police said that the man had disappeared into a crowded supermarket car park.

4. Valerie said she was more suspicious of people now.

5. The police said they were looking for a man in a brown jacket and jeans.

6. 'He put his hand in the drawer and tried to grab as much money as he could,' said Valerie.

7. 'There wasn't time to be frightened', she added.

8. 'We don't know the name of the man who chased him,' Valerie said.

9. 'He was quite tall and slim with a dark complexion,' she told the reporter.

2
Change sentences 2–4 into direct speech and sentences 5–7 into reported speech.

1. The reporter asked what time the robbery had happened.
   'What time did the robbery happen?' asked the reporter.

2. The policeman asked how many people there had been in the bank at the time.

3. The reporter asked what had happened.

4. The reporter asked Valerie who had chased the thief.

5. 'How much money did he get?' asked the reporter.

6. 'How do you feel now?' the reporter asked.

7. 'What was the man wearing?' asked the policeman.

Language Summary 2

Temporal changes to words

'I'm standing outside the Westland Bank where the raid took place **this** morning' said the reporter.
The reporter said that he was standing outside the Westland Bank where the raid took place **that** morning.
When direct speech is changed to reported speech, words that refer to time have to be changed.

3
Match the words on the left as used in direct speech with their reported speech equivalents on the right.

1. today — f that day
2. tomorrow — e the following day
3. yesterday — c the previous day
4. here — b there
5. now — a then
6. next — d shortly afterwards

Unit 5 Lesson 2

Language Summary 1

Reported speech: questions

Do you regret changing your job, Josie?' asked the reporter.
The reporter asked Josie *if/whether* she *regretted* changing her job.

Where there is no question word in the direct speech version, we used *if/whether* in reported speech.

1

Change sentences 2–5 into direct speech and sentences 6–8 into reported speech.

1 The reporter asked her if/whether she regretted changing her job. *'Do you regret changing your job, Josie?' asked the reporter.*

2 The inspector asked if any action had been taken to fight the fire before the fire service arrived.

3 The inspector asked whether sprinklers had been fitted.

4 The inspector asked if the cause of the fire had been identified.

5 The inspector asked if there was any other important information.

6 'Was the fire discovered by a person or by a mechanical device?' asked the inspector.

7 'Did somebody phone the fire service?' asked the inspector.

8 'Is there any evidence of damage to the structure?' asked the inspector.

Language Summary 2

Reporting verbs

'I'm sorry I didn't phone you when we got back to the station', said Josie to her husband.
Josie **apologised to** her husband **for** not **phoning** him.

The use of a reporting verb allows us to summarise part of the message when we use reported speech.

2

In each of the examples 1–7, use one of the reporting verbs from the box to complete a reported speech version of the sentence.

| apologise (for doing) | accuse (someone of doing) |
| admit (doing) | advise (someone to do) |
| thank (someone for doing) |
| promise (to do) | warn (someone not to do) |

1 'It's the owner's fault for not checking the fire alarm system', said an employee.
An employee *accused the owner of not checking the fire alarm.*

2 'It's true, I didn't check the fire alarm,' said the owner.
The owner _____

3 'I'm sorry that we took so long,' said the fire officer.

4 'Thank you anyway,' said the owner, 'you dealt with the fire very efficiently.'

5 'Don't go too near the fire, it's dangerous,' said the fire officer to the woman.

6 'If I were you,' said the fire officer to the man, 'I would have a fire alarm fitted.'

7 'I'll always phone you after fires in the future,' said Josie to her husband.

Vocabulary

3

Collocations:

Complete each of the phrases on the left with words from the list on the right.

1 To fight — a fog
2 Thick — b of smoke
3 Terrific — c a whistle
4 To sound — d a fire
5 To fan — e job
6 A cloud — f the flames
7 A nine-to-five — g heat

Unit 5 Lesson 3

Language Summary

Articles

The definite article

*There had been a number of thefts in **the** area.*
The definite article is used when there is only one of something.

*Then **the** first postcard arrived.*
It is also used when referring to something specific.

The indefinite article

*We got **a** postcard from France.*
The indefinite article is used for one of several.

***A** police officer has to wear a uniform.*
It is also used for a non-specific example.

Zero article

Crime doesn't pay.
Children often play jokes on people.
No article is used before abstract nouns and in general statements.

1

In each of these sentences put in either *a/an*, *the* or no article as appropriate.

1 Gordon used to stand in __the__ front garden by _____ pond.

2 One morning, Moira looked out of _____ window and saw that _____ gnome was missing.

3 _____ children who live in _____ area are always playing _____ jokes on people.

4 Moira reported _____ theft to _____ police, but they were unable to solve _____ crime.

5 _____ first postcard came from _____ France. It was _____ picture of Gordon with _____ suitcase on _____ beach.

6 She took _____ postcard to the police, but they just laughed and said that someone in _____ family was playing _____ joke on her.

7 One morning, Moira woke up to find Gordon was on _____ doorstep with _____ suitcase and _____ note.

2

In each of the spaces in this text from lesson 1 put either *a/an*, *the* or no article as appropriate. Do not look back at the original text until you have finished.

_____ daring bank robber got away with about £200 in _____ raid on _____ bank in Peterston yesterday. _____ incident happened just after midday at _____ Westland Bank in _____ High Street. According to _____ police, the man went up to _____ desk and asked _____ bank clerk to exchange _____ ten pound coins for _____ £10 note. As she was changing _____ money, he reached over and put his hand into _____ drawer. _____ bank clerk, Valerie Simpson, bravely tried to trap his fingers in _____ drawer, but he managed to grab _____ money and run away. _____ passer-by, who has not been identified, chased _____ man down _____ street and recovered some of _____ money which he had dropped, but _____ thief then disappeared into _____ crowded supermarket.

_____ Eyewitnesses described _____ thief as being middle-aged, about 5ft 10ins tall, slim, with short brown hair and with _____ pale complexion. He was wearing _____ blue lightweight jacket.

Now look back to check if your version is the same. If not, do you think your answers are possible alternatives?

Vocabulary

3

Question forms

In the following conversation, look carefully at the police officer's replies, and then fill in the interviewer's questions or comments.

Interviewer: *What exactly is your job?*

Police officer: I'm a community police officer.

Interviewer: _____

Police officer: I think visiting the schools makes me different from a normal police officer.

Interviewer: _____

Police officer: Well, yes, children do sometimes commit crimes, but it's often because they do things for a joke; they don't see it as crime.

Interviewer: _____

Police officer: Well, recently I've had to deal with the disappearance of several garden gnomes!

Interviewer: _____

Police officer: We usually just talk to them sternly about respect for other people's possessions.

80

Unit 6 Lesson 1

Language Summary 1

Relative pronouns

*There are things **which** have pictures of pineapples on them.*
Use **which** with things.

*Someone **who** collects ties is called a grabatologist.*
Use **who** with people.

*I have a friend **whose** kitchen is full of pineapples.*
Use **whose** with possessions and attributes.

1

Put either *who, whose* or *which* in each of the spaces in these sentences. In which of the sentences could the relative pronoun be omitted?

1 Mel Watson is a woman ___who___ has a strange collection in her kitchen.
2 The things _____ she collects all have some connection with pineapples.
3 She has over 100 objects _____ are decorated with pineapples.
4 She has a lot of friends _____ buy pineapple presents for her.
5 Collecting pineapples is something _____ she didn't deliberately set out to do.
6 I don't know anyone else _____ kitchen is full of pineapples.

Language Summary 2

Relative clauses

Defining relative clauses
*It's about a Japanese man **who collects matchbox labels**.*

Non-defining relative clauses
*Bill McDaniel, **who lives in California**, collects ties.*
*The Guinness Book of Records, **which contains details of world records**, is published every year.*
*Walter Kavanagh, **whose collection of credit cards is the largest in the world**, didn't have to pay for any of them.*

Extra information is put between the commas.

2

Rewrite each of these pairs of sentences as one complete sentence, using a relative pronoun.

1 The Guinness Book of Records contains details of world records. It is published every year.
   The Guinness Book of Records, which contains details of world records, is published every year.

2 Walter Kavanagh's nickname is Mr Plastic Fantastic. He collects credit cards.
   _____

3 Mel Watson has over 100 pineapples. She started her collection ten years ago.
   _____

4 Mel's favourite object is a brooch. It was given to her by her brother.
   _____

5 Mel's first object was a pineapple ice bucket. It is made of plastic.
   _____

Language Summary 3

That* and *which

*There are things **that/which** have pineapples on them.*
Use **that** or **which** when they are subjects of defining relative clauses.

*Mel has a collection of pineapples, **which** has over 100 objects.*
Use **which** and not **that** in non-defining relative clauses.

She became interested in objects connected with pineapples.
We can leave out *that* or *which* when they are objects in defining relative clauses.

3

The relative pronouns have been taken out of these sentences. Decide whether each one belongs to group A, B or C and put in the necessary pronouns.

A = *That* and *which* are both possible.
B = Only *which* is possible.
C = It is possible to leave out the pronoun.

1 Austin and Howard Mewse collect photographs _that/which_ have been signed by silent film stars. _A_
2 Hollywood, _____ is in California, was the home of most of the silent film stars. ____
3 It's the star's address _____ is the most important thing to find. ____
4 Once they have found the stars' addresses, they send photographs to them _____ they ask them to sign and return. ____
5 They are even interested in films _____ were not successful. ____
6 There are still some photographs _____ they haven't been able to find. ____

Unit 6 Lesson 2

Vocabulary

Adverbs and adjectives

*I go shopping very **occasionally**.*
*She is a **truly** compulsive shopper.*
*They are very **happily** married.*
Adverbs tell the manner, frequency or degree of actions and states.

1
Wordbuilding
Put in the missing form of these words in the spaces in the grid.

Noun	Adjective	Adverb
compulsion	compulsive	compulsively
	emotional	
impulse		
	occasional	
thrill		
	guilty	
		truly
		simply
	clinical	

2
In some of these sentences the wrong form of the word has been used. Decide whether each sentence contains a mistake or not and, if it does, write in the correct form.

1 To tell you the truth, I don't really believe in compulsive shopping. _Right_
2 He sometimes buys things on an impulsive. _Wrong._
   impulse
3 I am an occasionally shopper at the sales. _____
4 It is sometimes very thrill to buy something you can't afford. _____
5 Overspending leaves me feeling guilt. _____
6 I often react very emotionally. _____
7 It is not a simple case of addiction. _____
8 She was diagnosed as being in a state of clinically depression. _____

3
Make these notes into sentences of either type A: adverb + adjective + noun, or type B: adverb + adverb + adjective

1 She/true/compulsive/shopper
   She is a truly compulsive shopper.   _type A_
2 They/very/happy/married
   They are very happily married.   _type B_
3 He/obvious/serious/unhappy
4 She/severe/depressed/woman
5 I/strong/influenced/your argument
6 They/clear/impulsive/buyers
7 She/apparent/secret/addicted

Language Summary

Ways of giving advice

*You **should** cut up your credit card.*
You should + infinitive

*You **ought to** cut up your credit card.*
You ought to + infinitive

*You**'d better** cut up your credit card.*
You'd better + infinitive

***Why don't you** cut up your credit card?*
Why don't you + infinitive

***I suggest you** cut up your credit card.*
I suggest you + infinitive

***How about** cutting up your credit card?*
How about + -ing

4
Write sentences, using each of these forms, to give Joanne advice about her problem.

1 You should _____
2 You ought to _____
3 You'd better _____
4 Why don't you _____
5 How about _____
6 I suggest you _____
7 _____
8 _____

Unit 6 Lesson 3

Language Summary 1

First conditional

*If Cynthia **tells** the truth, Bob **will lose** his job.*
Use this form for things which seem likely.

*If I **lie**, how **can** I make people believe me?*
*If Cynthia **is called** as a witness, what **should** she say?*
Use other modal verbs to give extra meaning.

1

Use the notes to make first conditional sentences out of these pairs of ideas. Add words where necessary, remembering to use modal verbs where appropriate, and be careful not to repeat names.

1 Cynthia/tell/truth   Cynthia/husband/lose/job
   If Cynthia tells the truth, her husband will lose his job.

2 Cynthia/withdraw/statement everything/be/all right
   _____

3 Cynthia/be/call/witness   William/deny/steal/CD
   _____

4 William/say/accident   Cynthia/contradict/him
   _____

5 Bob/convince/Cynthia   Cynthia/withdraw/statement
   _____

6 Bob/lose/job   Bob/become/moody/depressed
   _____

7 Cynthia/stick/principles   Cynthia/ruin/Bob/career
   _____

8 Bob/become/moody/depressed Cynthia/unhappy
   _____

9 William/not tell/truth   judge/not believe/William
   _____

10 Cynthia/tell/lie   Cynthia/be/convincing
   _____

Language Summary 2

Second conditional

*If I **lied** under oath, I **would feel** terrible.*
Use this form for things which seem less likely, or which are impossible to change.

*If I **were** Cynthia, I **would tell** the truth.*
Use this form for hypothetical situations.

2

Finish each of the phrases 1–6 with one of the phrases a–f, putting appropriate words in the spaces, to form second conditional sentences.

1 If I saw someone shoplifting, __c__
2 If I _____ Cynthia, _____
3 If Cynthia _____ her story, _____
4 If I _____ in Bob's position, _____
5 If I _____ William, _____
6 If Jane _____ Bob the sack, _____

a The judge _____ not _____ her.
b I _____ that I had made a mistake.
c I __would tell__ a store detective.
d I _____ the truth.
e It _____ very unfair.
f I _____ very angry with Cynthia.

Vocabulary

3

Spelling

Decide if each of the following words is spelt correctly or not. If it is not, write the correct version in the space.

1 assessment   ✓   _____
2 questionnaire   ✗   questionnaire
3 iresistible   ___   _____
4 marketing   ___   _____
5 managment   ___   _____
6 received   ___   _____
7 tipical   ___   _____
8 arguement   ___   _____
9 employer   ___   _____
10 noticable   ___   _____
11 courageous   ___   _____
12 availibility   ___   _____

Unit 7 Lesson 1

Language Summary

Present participles

'It's no good,' he said, **putting on** his coat.
Seeing his hurt expression, Julia smiled apologetically.
We use present participles when two actions happen at the same time, or when one happens as an immediate result of another.

1
In each of these examples, make one sentence by using a present participle. The more important, or first, verb will usually take the subject.

1 'It's no good,' he said. He put on his coat as he said it.
   'It's no good,' he said, putting on his coat.

2 Julia sat in her mini. She drummed her fingers as she sat.

3 'I'm waiting for my husband,' she said. She was thinking fast.

4 'Time to move on,' she said to herself. She was heading out of town when she said it.

5 Julia changed into fourth gear. She smiled to herself as she did it.

6 'Need a hand, love?' said the man. He was peering through the car window.

2
Use a word from the box to form a present participle which will fit in each of the spaces in these sentences.

| walk | look | reach | ~~see~~ | speed |
| wave | swerve | give | | |

1 _Seeing_ his hurt expression, Julia smiled apologetically.

2 'Help! I've broken down!' she shouted, _____ her arms.

3 _____ at the man, Julie flicked down the lock on the door.

4 _____ up in spite of the rain, he headed down the lane.

5 Terry muttered, _____ to avoid a man _____ in the road.

6 _____ Julia his raincoat, the man rolled up his sleeves.

7 'You can trust me,' said the man, _____ in his pocket for his car keys.

Vocabulary

3
The box contains some verbs from the story. Divide them into three groups and write them in the table below. Some may belong to more than one group.

| frown | wander | tut | glance | peer | pat | step out |
| flick | groan | poke | shiver | hop | drum | nod |

Facial expression/ way of looking	Action/ movement	Sound
frown		

4
Look back at the text and the tapescript and decide whether these adjectives give a positive or a negative idea in the context of the story.

1 garish _negative_
2 burly _____
3 lurid _____
4 trustworthy _____
5 wary _____
6 swift _____
7 sleek _____
8 smoother _____

84

Unit 7 Lesson 2

Language Summary 1

Third conditional

The past conditional is used to talk about things which happened in the past and which cannot now be changed.

If the doctors **had believed** Maria's suspicions, there **wouldn't have been** the mix up.
= But the doctors didn't believe Maria's suspicions and the babies were mixed up.

1

Make past conditional sentences for each of these situations.

1 One of the babies lost his tag. The nurse gave him the wrong name.
   If *one of the babies hadn't lost his tag the nurse wouldn't have given him the wrong name.*

2 Maria told one of the doctors. The families know about the mix up.
   If _____

3 Blood tests were conducted. Maria was proved to be right.
   If _____

4 The families have decided to leave the boys as they are. Each family now has to adopt their son.
   If _____

5 There was a mix up. The boy born to poor parents is now rich.
   If _____

6 The parents decided not to swap the boys back. The rich boy has lost his inheritance.
   If _____

7 The doctors made a mistake. The babies were mixed up.
   If _____

Language Summary 2

Should(n't) have

We use the past form of the modal verb *should* to talk about things happening in the past which we think were wrong or which we regret, but which can't now be changed.

The doctors **should have** *believed Maria.*
= But they didn't believe her.

The doctors **shouldn't have** *made a mistake.*

We use *should/shouldn't* + infinitive to give our opinions about things in the present and future.

No child **should** *be kept away from its natural mother.*
= In my opinion.

2

Use the information from the story to complete these sentences using *should/shouldn't have* + past participle.

1 The doctors *shouldn't have allowed* such a mistake to happen.
2 The hospital _____ so badly organised.
3 The babies _____ the same name tag.
4 The nurse _____ the baby a new tag.
5 The nurse _____ the babies' identities.
6 The clinic _____ to Maria's suspicions.
7 Blood tests _____ earlier.
8 The boys _____ back when they were still babies.

3

Use *should/shouldn't* + infinitive to give your opinions about the problem of the boys' future.

1 *I think the boys should/shouldn't be told about the mix-up.*
2 _____
3 _____
4 _____
5 _____
6 _____
7 _____

Unit 7 Lesson 3

Language Summary

Revision of passives: passive form of verbs

We use the passive form of verbs when we do not know, or do not want to say, who or what is the subject of the sentence.

*The coat **had been made** somewhere in South America.*
It is not important who made it.
*The speed with which urban myths **are passed on** is an issue of concern.*
We don't know who they are passed on by.

Passive form of modal verbs

*Urban myths **mustn't be taken** too seriously.*
*The story **might have been started** by rivals.*
Modal verbs in the passive are followed by **be** in the present and **have been** in the past, and the past participle.

1
Change the verbs in these sentences from the active to the passive form.

1 Someone is going to publish an important report.
 An important report is going to be published.

2 They brought in an expert to save the situation.

3 A snake bit a woman customer.

4 They are investigating the story.

5 The story baffled the detectives.

6 Someone eventually bought the footballer for a large sum of money.

7 People are likely to repeat the most outrageous stories.

8 The story said that they made the bubblegum from spiders' eggs.

9 Commercial rivals probably started the stories.

10 A newspaper in Florida published the story.

2
Change the verbs in these sentences from the active to the passive form.

1 People mustn't take urban myths too seriously.
 Urban myths mustn't be taken too seriously

2 Someone might have started the story innocently.

3 They should make a public announcement.

4 Someone ought to have denied the story at the outset.

5 A viper can't have laid eggs in the pocket.

6 Someone has to show that the story is untrue.

7 They could neither prove nor disprove the story.

8 Urban myths can cause serious economic problems.

Vocabulary

3
The words on the left are from the passage. Match each one with a word of similar meaning from the list on the right.

1 retire — confuse
2 soar — proof
3 baffle — stop working
4 plunge — exaggerated
5 spot — rise quickly
6 combat — fall quickly
7 outrageous — fight
8 authentication — notice

4
Write the correct past participle for each of the verbs on the left.

1 wear   *worn*
2 find   _____
3 mistake _____
4 frighten _____
5 lay   _____
6 spread _____
7 target _____
8 combat _____

Unit 8 Lesson 1

Language Summary 1

Comparative forms of adjectives

*Girl babies are **more sensitive** to touch **than** boys.*
Adjectives with many syllables take *more*.

*Girls are **closer** to their mothers **than** boys.*
Adjectives with only one syllable take the suffix *-er*.

1
Write the comparative forms of these adjectives.

long	_longer_	easy	_____
mobile	_____	skilful	_____
wet	_____	methodical	_____
aggressive	_____	fine	_____
alike	_____	likely	_____

2
Match a comparative adjective from activity 1 to each of these rules.

1 Add a suffix to the adjective. eg. _longer_
2 Double the final consonant and add a suffix. eg. _____
3 Add one letter to the adjective. eg. _____
4 Change one letter and add a suffix. eg. _____
5 Put a modifying word before the adjective. eg. _____

Language Summary 2

Comparisons of equality and inequality.

Comparisons of equality
*Boys are **as interested** in objects **as** they are in people.*

Comparisons of inequality
*Boys are **not as sensitive** to touch **as** girls.*
This form can be used with all adjectives after the verb *to be*.

*Men become **less aggressive than** women as they grow older.*
This form can be used with all adjectives after the verb *to become/to get*.

3
Find information from the reading on page 48 to complete these sentences with *as/as* or *not as/as*. Then find two more of your own.

1 Baby boys are _not as_ sensitive to touch _as_ baby girls.
2 Baby boys are _____ interested in objects _____ in people.
3 Girls at school are _____ aggressive _____ boys.
4 Boys at school are _____ good at reading _____ girls.
5 _____
6 _____

Language Summary 3

Comparison of adverbs

*Girls learn to read **more quickly than** boys.*
Adverbs ending in *-ly* take *more*.

*Boys take a year **longer than** girls.*
Some adverbs have the same form as the adjective and take *-er*.

4
Think of someone you know very well (eg. brother/sister/best friend) and write sentences comparing yourself with that person using some of the adverbs from the box.

> clearly   aggressively   confidently   slowly
> quickly   hard   carefully   badly   beautifully
> regularly   neatly   well   easily   fast

1 _I work much harder than my brother does._
2 _I don't read as quickly as he does._
3 _____
4 _____
5 _____
6 _____
7 _____

Vocabulary

5
Text organisation: linking words

Choose the correct alternative from the words in brackets.

It is known (which/<u>that</u>) the brain is very complex. Recent studies of the brain have shown (that/what) it divides into two hemispheres, (for example/namely) right and left, (and/but) that (although/however) there are other parts of the brain involved in its overall function, it is the right and left hemispheres that are most important. It is (now/presently) believed that the right and left hemispheres have very different functions; (the former/the one) deals with spatial relationships (like/such as) recognising faces, and (the latter/the later) deals with logical thinking. (However/Surprisingly) these facts were discovered (on/through) the study of people who had suffered brain damage and had (therefore/so) lost certain functions of their brains.

Unit 8 Lesson 2

Language Summary

Conditional sentences in reported speech

First conditional
'If you **look** into the bag, you **will be able to** tell which pebble I took,' said the girl.
The girl said that **if** he **looked** into the bag he **would be able to** tell which pebble she had taken.
When we report conditionals, the present tense changes to the past and **will** changes to **would**.

Second conditional
'If you **used** lateral thinking you **would** find a solution,' said the writer.
The writer said that if you **used** lateral thinking you **would** find a solution.
When we report conditionals, the past tense does not change and **would** remains **would**.

Third conditional
'If the money lender **had been** honest she **would have had** only a fifty-fifty chance.'
When we report conditionals, the past perfect does not change and **would have** remains **would have**.

1

Change each of these sentences into reported speech.

1 'If you choose the white pebble, your father's debt will be cancelled,' said the money lender.
   The money lender said that if she chose the white pebble, her father's debt would be cancelled.

2 'If the girl does not take a pebble, her father will go to prison,' said the storyteller.

3 'I would cancel the debt if I could have the girl instead,' said the money lender.

4 'What would you have told the girl to do, if you had had to advise her?' asked the teacher.

2

Change each of these sentences into direct speech.

1 The money lender said that if she chose the white pebble she would stay with her father.
   'If you choose the white pebble, you will stay with your father,' said the money lender.

2 The money lender said that if she refused to pick out a pebble, her father would be thrown in jail.

3 The teacher asked us what we would do if we were in a similar situation.

4 John said that if the girl hadn't noticed that the money lender was cheating, there would have been no story.

Vocabulary

3
Wordbuilding

In the square there are 11 verbs from this lesson. Find them and then complete the chart below. Where more than one adjective is possible, what is the difference between the two?

D	X	G	A	E	F	I	D	E	N	C
E	X	P	L	O	R	E	U	C	P	O
F	R	H	W	P	I	A	A	R	R	M
I	E	I	M	A	G	I	N	E	O	P
N	A	A	O	O	H	N	A	A	M	A
E	S	K	S	L	T	F	L	T	I	R
V	O	A	G	R	E	E	Y	E	S	E
S	N	M	B	B	N	Q	S	A	E	Y
S	T	A	R	V	E	U	E	E	A	E

Verb	Noun	Adjective
agree	agreement	agreed/agreeable

Unit 8 Lesson 3

Language Summary

Verbs with infinitive and *-ing* form

*I'm **unable to remember** names.*
Some verbs are always followed by an infinitive.

*I **enjoy** (doing) memory tests.*
Some verbs are always followed by the *-ing* form or a noun.

***Try** to remember the number.*
= Please do it, it's important.
***Try** remembering the number.*
= It would be a good idea.
Some verbs can be followed by either the infinitive or the *-ing* form.

*I **remembered** to buy the bread.*
In this sentence 'to go' happened after 'I remembered'.
*I **remembered** buying the bread.*
In this sentence, 'going' happened before 'I remembered'.
Sometimes the choice of infinitive or *-ing* form can change the meaning.

1

Choose the correct form from the alternatives in brackets.

1. Are you able (to memorise/memorising) lists of numbers?
2. Do you remember (to go/going) to the seaside when you were young?
3. The article suggests (to memorise/memorising) images rather than words.
4. I must remember (to go/going) shopping on my way home this evening.
5. You can't improve your memory without (to make/making) an effort.
6. I am not capable of (to repeat/repeating) somebody's words without (to change/changing) them.
7. The article recommends (to create/creating) a visual image of words.
8. (To remember/Remembering) is a learned skill that demands hard work.

2

Divide words from the box into the two groups below.

A Those usually followed by an infinitive
B Those usually followed by the *-ing* form

> admit   afford   avoid   agree   dare   resist
> face   offer   miss   intend   regret   finish   want
> risk   mention   forgive   decide   manage   postpone
> expect   consider   refuse   hope   hesitate

3

Using the verb in brackets, complete each of these sentences with either an infinitive or a preposition and the *-ing* form.

1. You need a strategy *for improving* your memory. (improve)
2. I am better _____ names than numbers. (remember)
3. Actors say there is no quick way _____ their lines. (learn)
4. Memory techniques work _____ a context for the material. (provide)
5. Mark Twain was one of the first people _____ (devise) a system _____ (remember) his speeches.
6. It is quite possible _____ (create) a useful image and _____ (have) a conversation at the same time.

Vocabulary

4

Use either a prefix or a suffix (or both!) from the boxes to make as many new words as possible from those in the list.

Prefixes	Suffixes
in im out re un	ize ful able less

1. ability _____
2. possible _____
3. call _____
4. standing _____
5. able _____
6. visual _____
7. remark _____
8. familiar _____
9. organ _____
10. use _____

Unit 9 Lesson 1

Language Summary 1

Reflexive verbs

A confident person will always **hold themselves** *upright.*
Some verbs take a direct reflexive pronoun.
The way out of the maze of failure is to **believe in yourself**.
Other verbs take a preposition and pronoun.

1

Put the correct reflexive pronoun from the box in each of the spaces in these sentences. Add a preposition where necessary.
Try to use each pronoun at least once.

| myself yourself himself herself itself |
| yourselves ourselves themselves |

1 When you are aware *of yourself* you are confident.
2 You should try to convince _____ of your abilities.
3 I always pride _____ on my patience.
4 She shouldn't deny _____ the good things in life.
5 You don't have to go in a group, some of you could go _____ .
6 There's no point in getting annoyed _____ .
7 People can be what they want if they have confidence _____ .
8 It's important to stand up _____ in an argument.
9 The important thing in life is to enjoy _____ .

Language Summary 2

Verb and preposition combinations

Believe in *yourself.*
Be **aware of** *yourself.*
Some verbs take prepositions.

2

Put a preposition in each of the sentences, or put – if it is unnecessary.

1 Is your friend losing interest *in* you?
2 You should start _____ going out more often.
3 Do you deserve _____ a rise at work?
4 Can you give me the reason _____ your decision?
5 She accused him _____ trying to cheat her.
6 I agree _____ you about that problem.
7 I need to convince him _____ my honesty.
8 They started to argue _____ something trivial.
9 He denied _____ making a mistake.
10 I was keen to accomplish _____ something.

Vocabulary

3

Match the verb from the list on the left with the words from the list on the right to make an idiomatic phrase.

1 To work	over the top
2 To make	your time
3 To bring up	an act
4 To do	a fuss
5 To get	your ground
6 To make up	your best
7 To put on	the subject
8 To go	something out
9 To take	an excuse
10 To stand	your own way

4

Each line of the following passage contains one spelling mistake. Underline the misspelt word and write the correct version in the space at the end of the line.

How people <u>demestrate</u> self-confidence?   *demonstrate*
There are obvious signs, often in body langage   _____
and in the way a person beheaves towards others.   _____
Confident people will hold themselfs upright   _____
and will learn forward to listen. They don't rush   _____
in to fil silences in conversations, they can take   _____
time to think about what they want to say without   _____
being affraid of appearing hesitant. And they   _____
always appear relaxt, wearing whatever they like   _____
and sitting comftably in their chairs.   _____

Unit 9 Lesson 2

Language Summary 1

Modal verbs: *can/be able to*

You **can do** it.
Can is followed by an infinitive.

I'll never **be able to pass** this exam.
Can has no infinitive or participle. *Be able to* is used in these contexts.

1

In these sentences, use *can* where this is possible and a form of *be able to* where it is not.

1 He's so frightened of heights, he hasn't _been able to_ get in a plane.
2 If I want, I _can_ do anything.
3 You _____ do anything you want, but you have to _____ believe in yourself.
4 _____ try new things is an important gift.
5 Immediately after the accident, he _____ fly at all.
6 Now he wants to find out what other sports he _____ take part in.
7 I've never _____ go up tall buildings.
8 You need _____ try new things.
9 I _____ understand how frightened he was when he first tried hang-gliding.
10 Not _____ see hasn't stopped John from enjoying life.
11 If positive thinking _____ solve all the world's problems, life would be much easier.
12 Although Barbara _____ understand John's fears, she wants him _____ enjoy all the things he did before the accident.

Language Summary 2

Modal verbs: *need/don't need/needn't*

I **needed** something to help me overcome my fear of heights.
Positive thinking is all you **need** to improve your life.
Need can be a normal verb or a modal auxiliary (especially in the negative).

There's no **need** for you to fail.
Need is also used as a noun.

2

Rewrite each of these sentences using a different form of *need* as suggested by the word at the beginning.

1 You don't need to fail all the time.
   You _needn't fail all the time._
2 You needn't give up just because you're afraid.
   There's _____
3 There's no need to think you will fail; expect to succeed instead.
   You don't _____
4 There's no need to undervalue your abilities.
   You _____
5 You needn't be afraid of making mistakes.
   There's _____
6 You needn't go on thinking negative thoughts.
   There's _____
7 You don't need to worry about whether you are successful or not.
   There's _____

Vocabulary

3

Even though

Link each of these pairs of ideas into a sentence using *even though*.

1 Very good pilot. Crashed plane.
   Even though he was a very good pilot, he crashed the plane.
2 John not killed in accident. Lost his sight.
   _____
3 John used to fly plane. Now afraid of heights.
   _____
4 John blind. Learnt to hang-glide.
   _____
5 They are disabled. Club teaches things they want to do.
   _____
6 Didn't believe he could do it. Wife encouraged him to try.
   _____
7 Very scared. First time felt fantastic.
   _____

Unit 9 Lesson 3

Language Summary 1

Adverbs of frequency

*Have you **ever** been in this situation?*
Adverbs of frequency can come between the subject and verb.

*I have **never** been able to say what I really feel.*
They can also come after the auxiliary and before the main verb.

Adverbs of manner

*People will think you are just acting **emotionally**.*
*He spoke to her **angrily**.*
Adverbs of manner come after the subject and verb, and usually after the object.

1

Decide if the adverbs in the box are:

Type A = Frequency   Type B = Manner

frequently	_A_	rudely	_B_	usually	___
never	___	politely	___	generally	___
assertively	___	rarely	___	always	___
confidently	___	sometimes	___	nervously	___
occasionally	___	resentfully	___	successfully	___
normally	___	helpfully	___	seldom	___

Choose two of the adverbs from the box to add to each of these sentences.

1 I speak to my boss.
   I usually speak to my boss politely.

2 He answers me.

3 'I go dancing,' she said.

4 She drives her car.

5 'I accept invitations,' he said.

6 'You make me feel stupid,' she said.

Language Summary 2

It's time + past tense (subjunctive)
*It's time you **said** something.*
I don't say anything.

This form is used to talk about things that should have happened already and to give strong advice.

2

Respond to each of these statements using *it's time*.

1 I don't show my feelings enough.
   It's time you showed your feelings more.

2 I never tell my friend when I'm angry with her.

3 I never complain in restaurants when the service is bad.

4 I'm always losing my temper.

5 I don't know how to apologise.

6 I never admit when I'm wrong.

Vocabulary

Inversion

Not only... but
__Not only__ is the restaurant dirty, __but__ the food is awful too!
Not only... but is used to add emphasis to what is being said.
After *not only* the subject and verb are inverted.

3

Rewrite each of these sentences using the *not only* form.

1 This restaurant is dirty. The food is awful.
   Not only is this restaurant dirty, but the food is awful.

2 This restaurant is very expensive. The waiters are rude.

3 The chairs are uncomfortable. The tablecloth is dirty.

4 This shop is expensive. The assistants are unhelpful.

5 The assistants are unhelpful. The manager is rude.

6 The counsellor is well qualified. His fees are reasonable.

7 His fees are very reasonable. He's helped a lot of people.

8 He's helped a lot of people. He appeared on TV last year.

9 He appeared on TV last year. He's also written a book.

Unit 10 Lesson 1

Language Summary 1

Time clauses with *before*, *after*, and *once*

Before leaving the house, he put the letter in his pocket.
Before + second action + first action.

After re-reading the letter, she put it back in her handbag.
After + first action + second action.

Once Jack had left for the foundry, Edna woke Enoch.
Once + first action + second action.

1

Put *before*, *after* or *once* in each of these sentences based on the story, and then complete the missing information.

1 *Once* Jack was up, his wife put his *breakfast on the table.*
2 _____ leaving the house, Jack called _____
3 _____ changing his clothes, Jack walked to _____
4 _____ getting on the train, Jack met _____
5 _____ Enoch had finished his breakfast, he went _____
6 _____ leaving the house, Edna packed _____

Language Summary 2

Clauses with *having*

Having worked in the same factory, they had 'fallen for each other'.
Having + first action + subject + second action.

2

Rewrite each of these sentences using a clause beginning with *having*.

1 Jack had taken off his overalls and now wore a suit.
   Having taken off his overalls, Jack now wore a suit.
2 Edna gave Enoch his breakfast and then watched him eat it.
3 Before sending him to school, Edna gave Enoch sixpence.
4 Once she had said goodbye to Enoch, Edna packed her bags.
5 Edna had been married for ten years and wanted a change.

Language Summary 3

Past intentions: past continuous for future in the past

*They **were intending** to act.*
This tells us what they intended to do at a time in the past.

3

Write a sentence using each of the verbs in the box about the intentions of Jack and Edna when they woke up that morning. You can use your imagination as well as information from the story.

| plan   intend   hope   go   mean |
| think of (+ -ing)   look forward to (+ -ing) |

Jack
1 *He was intending to leave his wife.*
2 *He wasn't planning to go to ...*
3 _____
4 _____
5 _____

Edna
1 *She was going to leave her husband.*
2 *She was thinking of staying with ...*
3 _____
4 _____
5 _____

Vocabulary

4

Match words from the text on page 61 with the word or phrase below which is closest in meaning.

| upset   irritated   tackling   dumb |
| muted   dull   bothering |

1 unable to speak   *dumb*
2 boring   _____
3 trying to solve   _____
4 shared   _____
5 unhappy   _____
6 made angry   _____
7 worrying   _____

Which words could you use in these phrases?

a It's not worth _____ about.
b It was a _____ film.
c Their dislike was _____.
d She was _____ a hard problem.
e She was _____ by his lack of concern.

Unit 10 Lesson 2

Language Summary 1

Conjunctions: *If* replacements (positive)

If/As long as/Provided they didn't find out, they wouldn't be angry.
Depends on the condition.

When/As soon as they found out, they'd be angry.
Depends on the time.

Whether they found out ***or not***, they'd be angry.
Doesn't depend on condition or time.

1
Put one of the conjunctions from the box into each of the spaces in the sentences about Enoch's experience.

| as soon as | whether ... or not |
| as long as | provided |

1 *As soon as* it got dark, he switched on the light.
2 His mother should have been home by then, _____ she'd missed the bus or not.
3 He would get out of the armchair _____ he heard his father arriving.
4 _____ he had gone upstairs or not, he wouldn't have found any cigarettes.
5 He drew the curtains _____ it got dark.
6 _____ he could keep warm, he was happy to sleep on the sofa.
7 _____ they came home soon, he wouldn't have to go upstairs alone.
8 _____ they didn't come back tonight, he wouldn't have to go to school in the morning.

Language Summary 2

Conjunctions: *If* replacements (negative)

If you ***don't go*** to bed, you'll be tired tomorrow.
If + negative verb.

Unless you ***go*** to bed, you'll be tired tomorrow.
Unless + positive verb.

Go to bed, ***otherwise*** you'll be tired tomorrow.
Otherwise = *if not*.

2
Rewrite each of the sentences using the new conjunction in brackets, but keeping the meaning the same.

1 Unless they came back, he'd have to sleep downstairs.
   If they didn't come back, he'd have to sleep downstairs.

2 He decided to sleep under the carpet, otherwise he would be very cold. (Unless)
   _____

3 He turned the gas fire down, otherwise he would run out of gas. (If)
   _____

4 Unless he was sitting on his father's knee, he wasn't allowed to use that chair. (If)
   _____

5 If he didn't keep away from the fire, he would burn his legs. (Unless)
   _____

6 Without concentrating, he couldn't remember what his parents looked like. (Unless)
   _____

7 If he didn't keep the gas fire burning, he'd be cold in the night. (Otherwise)
   _____

8 He watched the television, otherwise he'd feel lonely. (If)
   _____

Language Summary 3

Conjunctions: *although* and *despite/in spite of*

Although he had eaten some bread and jam, he was still hungry.
Although + subject + verb.

Despite/In spite of eating the bread and jam, he was still hungry.
Despite/In spite of + *-ing*

Despite/In spite of the bread and jam, he was still hungry.
Despite/In spite of + noun.

3
Use the words in brackets to complete the sentences in the context of Enoch's story.

1 Although *he looked everywhere*, he couldn't find a cigarette. (look)
2 Despite *looking everywhere*, he couldn't find any cigarettes. (look)
3 Although _____, he didn't turn it off. (television)
4 Despite _____, he didn't go upstairs. (blanket)
5 Although _____, he drank it. (tea)
6 Despite _____, he hoped his parents were all right. (enjoy himself)
7 In spite of _____, he was quite sensible. (age)

Unit 10 Lesson 3

Language Summary 1

Present wishes

I **wish** my parents **were** here.
But they aren't here.

He **wishes** he **had** some cigarettes.
But he hasn't any cigarettes.

I **wish** I **could** go to school tomorrow.
But he can't go.

He **wishes** he **hadn't cried** in front of his grandmother.
But he did cry in front of her.

To talk about present wishes we use wish and the past simple.

1

These sentences tell us about Enoch's feelings the next morning. Change each sentence so that it begins with *wish* but don't change the meaning.

1 He would like his parents to come home.
   He wishes his parents would come home.

2 He is disappointed that he can't have a cooked breakfast.
   He wishes _____

3 He is sorry that he isn't going to school today.
   He wishes _____

4 It is a pity his grandma lives so far away.
   He _____

5 He is sorry that he hasn't got more money.
   _____

6 He would like to be able to live in the house alone.
   _____

7 It's a nuisance that he has no money for gas.
   _____

8 It would be nice to be old enough to live alone.
   _____

9 He would be pleased if one of his friends came to see him.
   _____

10 It would be good if it stopped raining.
   _____

Language Summary 2

Past regrets

I **wish** I **hadn't** cried in front of his grandmother.
But I did cry in front of her.

I **wish** they **hadn't left** me.
But they did leave me.

To talk about past regrets we use wish and the past perfect.

2

Looking back over the story, make a list of things that Enoch regrets about his experience. Use the words in brackets as ideas and then go on to find your own examples.

1 He wishes *he hadn't cried in front of his grandma.*
  (cry/grandma)

2 He wishes _____
  (lock/door)

3 He _____
  (go/neighbours)

4 _____
  (sleep/bed)

5 _____
  (be/frightened)

6 _____
7 _____
8 _____
9 _____
10 _____

3

Look at the second text on page 65 and say what the following words refer to.

1 they (line 4) *his parents*
2 they (line 6) _____
3 They (line 17) _____
4 it (line 20) _____
5 They (line 23) _____
6 them (line 27) _____
7 It (line 37) _____
8 They (line 40) _____
9 them (line 44) _____
10 they (line 45) _____

95